# Barriers to Democracy

# Barriers to Democracy

THE OTHER SIDE OF SOCIAL CAPITAL
IN PALESTINE AND THE ARAB WORLD

*Amaney A. Jamal*

PRINCETON UNIVERSITY PRESS
PRINCETON AND OXFORD

Published by Princeton University Press, 41 William Street, Princeton, New Jersey 08540

In the United Kingdom: Princeton University Press, 3 Market Place, Woodstock, Oxfordshire OX20 1SY

British Library Cataloging-in-Publication Data is available

This book has been composed in Times Ten.

Printed on acid-free paper. ∞

press.princeton.edu

Printed in the United States of America

10  9  8  7  6  5  4  3  2

Library of Congress Cataloging-in-Publication Data
Jamal, Amaney A., 1970–
    Barriers to democracy : the other side of social capital in Palestine and the Arab world /
Amaney A. Jamal.
        p. cm.
    Includes bibliographical references and index.
    ISBN-13: 978-0-691-12727-9 (hardcover : alk. paper)
    ISBN-10: 0-691-12727-1 (hardcover : alk. paper)
      1. Civil society—Arab countries. 2. Civil society—West Bank. 3. Political
participation—Arab countries. 4. Political participation—West Bank. 5. Social capital
(Sociology)—Arab countries. 6. Social capital (Sociology)—West Bank. 7. Associations,
institutions, etc.—Arab countries. 8. Associations, institutions, etc.—West Bank.
9. Authoritarianism—Arab countries. 10. Authoritarianism—West Bank.   I. Title.
    JQ1850.A91J346   2007
    300.917′4927—dc22                                                    2006030034

The tyrant calls for sweet wine from sour grapes.
—Kahlil Gibran

# Contents

# Illustrations

# Preface

In 1999, I set out toward Palestine to understand the relationship between civic associations and democracy. At the time, this theme was receiving much attention in academic, scholarly, and policy debates. Although several other issues were on the minds of ordinary Palestinians—especially the Israeli Occupation and deteriorating economic conditions—I continued to examine the relationship between civic associations and democratic forms of citizenship. I found that state-society relations affected the quality of democratic forms of civic engagement. In nations that are governed by nondemocratic regimes, civic associations can bolster forms of democratic civic engagement, but they may also reproduce factors that lend support to authoritarian rule more broadly. This book uncovers the dynamic relationship between regime and society and its linkages to democratic patterns of civic engagement in the context of the West Bank.

ACKNOWLEDGMENTS

This book would not have been possible without the help and support of my advisers, colleagues, friends, and family. I am indebted to many people for their support, feedback, and guidance throughout the research phase and writing process of this book.

I extend special thanks and recognition to my advisers at the University of Michigan: Jennifer Widner, Pradeep Chhibber, Ann Lin, Mark Tessler, and Juan Cole. My colleagues at Princeton University have been equally supportive. Nancy Bermeo, Jeff Herbst, Atul Kohli, and Deborah Yashar have all provided substantial feedback and insightful remarks on this project. Several people read the manuscript for this book, and in particular I would like to thank Lisa Anderson, Ellen Lust-Okar, and Irfan Nooruddin for their patience and generous support. I also thank Gary Bass, Laurie Brand, Christina Davis, Deborah Gerner, Kosuke Imai, David Lewis, and Joshua Tucker for their useful comments and suggestions at various points during this research project. I have had the unique opportunity to present this work at several workshops, and I thank all workshop participants and organizers for their invitations: Lisa Wedeen and Carles Boix at the University of Chicago, Ellen Lust-Okar at Yale, Carl Brown at Princeton, and John Carey and Gene Garthwaite at Dartmouth College.

Input from my colleagues and friends has been instrumental, not only to my writing of the manuscript itself, but also to my scholarly development.

This book has paved the way to many solid collegiate ties and enduring friendships. I found great comfort and wonderful people in the dissertation room, at the computer lab, and over coffee. More importantly, I left Michigan with lifelong friendships. Khristina Haddad, Claudio Holzner, Ryan Hudson, Manal Jamal, Dulcey Simpkins, Joan Sitomor, Marek Steedman, and Tasha Philpot—I will always remember your generosity, support, and time. I also want to thank all the researchers who worked with me on this project: Tonya Howe, Alexandra Kobishyn, Susan Song, and Olga Lysenko and the researchers from al-Najah and Birzeit Universities for their invaluable research assistance, and Simon Samoeil for his helpful transliterations. I am also grateful to Chuck Myers, my editor at Princeton University Press, who has been enthusiastic and supportive of my project from the very start. I also wish to thank the anonymous reviewers who provided very valuable comments during the revision and submission processes.

I am further indebted to the generous support of the Jerusalem Media and Communications Center in Jerusalem and that of Dr. Ghassan al-Khatib in particular. Dr. al-Khatib endorsed and supported my project from the beginning and worked with me to ensure that my surveys were handled professionally and thoughtfully. I also wish to thank all the associational leaders in Palestine and Morocco who agreed to participate in this project. I was fortunate to have received ample financial support for this project, and I would especially like to thank the International Institute at the University of Michigan, the Rackham Graduate School at the University of Michigan, the Columbia University Department of Political Science, the Princeton University Department of Politics, and the University Committee on Research in the Humanities and Social Sciences at Princeton University.

This book could not have been possible without the love and care of my family. Nidal Jamal, Nijma Saadeddin, Alaeddine Saadeddin, Randa Jamal, and Eman Jamal all provided much-needed household skills, day care expertise, and personal reassurance. Without the support and commitment of my husband and children I could not have completed this project. I thank my husband, Helmi, for his ongoing enthusiastic and caring support of my research endeavors. My three daughters, Asma, Lina, and Ayah, remain enamored with my research expeditions. For years, with loving reinforcement, they have asked me, "Is your book done yet?" Though they never fully comprehended the magnitude of writing a book, they completely understood the labor that went into it.

Finally, I would like to dedicate this book in loving memory to my father, Ahmad Jamal. Your dream as an immigrant to this country was to see your children educated. You would have been proud.

# Note to the Reader

The Arabic language is transliterated using the standards of the *International Journal of Middle East Studies* (IJMES).

## ABBREVIATIONS AND ACRONYMS

| | |
|---|---|
| CSOs | civil society organizations |
| DFLP | Democratic Front for the Liberation of Palestine |
| DP | Déclaration Préalable |
| Fatah | Palestinian National Liberation Movement |
| FTUJ | Federation of Trade Unions in Jordan |
| GDP | gross domestic product |
| GFJW | General Federation of Jordanian Women |
| GNP | gross national product |
| GUVS | General Union of Voluntary Societies (Jordan) |
| NDP | National Democratic Party (Egypt) |
| NGOs | nongovernmental organizations |
| PFLP | Popular Front for the Liberation of Palestine |
| PI | Istiqlal Party (Morocco) |
| PLC | Palestinian Legislative Council |
| PLO | Palestine Liberation Organization |
| PMD | Public Monitoring Department (Palestine) |
| PNA | Palestinian National Authority |
| PVOs | private voluntary organizations |
| RTM | Radio-Television Marocaine |
| TM | Transparency Maroc |
| UNFP | The National Union of Popular Forces (Morocco) |
| USFP | Socialist Union of Popular Forces (Morocco) |
| WUJ | Women's Union in Jordan |

Barriers to Democracy

# CHAPTER ONE

# Introduction: Democratic Outcomes and Associational Life

ACROSS THE THIRD WORLD, the discourse on civil society has remained a key feature of democracy promotion initiatives. Scholars evaluating the potential for democracy in these developing states and activists seeking to effect democratic reforms have focused much of their attention on civic associations. They argue that civil societies help to hold states accountable, represent citizen interests, channel and mediate mass concerns, bolster an environment of pluralism and trust, and socialize members to the behavior required for successful democracies.[1]

International organizations have also clearly accepted the premise that strong civic groups will promote democratization and political stability, and they have enthusiastically funded projects deemed useful for enhancing activities leading to civil society. For over a decade now, international organizations have tried to influence democratization through civil societies. Such organizations have the tools—money, influence, and the backing of the international community—to affect the growth of civic associations around the world. In 1990 there were an estimated six thousand international nongovernmental organizations (NGOs); by 1999 that number had grown to twenty-six thousand (World Bank, 2000). Of World Bank–financed projects approved in the fiscal year 1995, for instance, 41% involved NGOs compared with an average of 6% for projects approved between 1973 and 1988.[2] According to Amy Hawthorne, "The majority of [US] democracy aid for the Middle East from 1991–2001—$150 million dollars—went to projects classified as civil society strengthening."[3]

---

[1]Ottaway and Carothers, *Funding Virtue;* Hoogh and Stolle, *Generating Social Capital;* Henderson, *Building Democracy in Contemporary Russia;* May and Milton, *(Un)civil Societies;* Krishna, "Enhancing Political Participation in Democracies"; Kenneth Newton, "Trust, Social Capital, Civil Society, and Democracy," *International Political Science Review* (2001); Letki, "Socialization for Participation?"; Hearn, "Aiding Democracy?"; Finkel, "Can Democracy Be Taught?"; Gibson, "Social Networks"; John Clark, "The State"; Hadi, "Decentralized Cooperation"; Blair, "Donors, Democratization, and Civil Society"; World Bank, *National Endowment;* Global Policy Organization (1996); Abu 'Amr, "Pluralism and Palestinians"; Norton and Ibrahim, "The Future of Civil Society in the Middle East"; Ibrahim, "Democratization in the Arab World"; Huntington, *The Third Wave.*

[2]World Bank, "New Paths to Social Development."

[3]Hawthorne, "Middle Eastern Democracy."

Further, a significant number of the Middle East Partnership Initiative (MEPI) programs implemented in 2002 channeled their monies to civil society programs. If participation in civic associations grows, the argument goes, so too will democratic forms of government—and all from grass-roots efforts.

In the West Bank, ruled ostensibly by the Palestinian National Authority (PNA) since 1993, Palestinian association leaders are no exception to the worldwide enthusiasts who have applauded the potential democratizing role of civil society. Leaders emphasized their commitment to achieving social improvement through associations. As a Palestinian association leader commented in 1999, "These goals [building civic associations] are important so that we can accomplish an overall development and obtain the building of a democratic society that offers all the opportunities in work and education and the availability of all the services and social equality."[4]

These leaders were enthusiastic because associational life in Western democracies reinforces patterns of civic engagement that mediate democratic practices and forms of participation. Several key features of these democratic institutions are directly related to the viability of civic organizations. Democratic governments, for instance, do not normally promote their own interests at the expense of the public, and citizens have avenues of political recourse for holding public officials accountable for misuse of public office for personal gain. Citizens of democratic polities, moreover, can participate in both politics and an associational life that is directly political. Implicit in current examinations of the effectiveness of associational life for the promotion of attitudes, activities, and belief systems favorable to the sustenance of democracies, however, is the understanding that associations and their immediate surroundings are supported by existing democratic structures, laws, and practices.[5]

Yet these same Palestinian leaders also expressed concern about the ability of civil society to influence democratic change. According to their accounts, the PNA was by 1999 creating conditions that stifled their progress. More broadly, many scholars of the rest of the Arab world began to question whether an active and vibrant civic polity would induce democratic change at all.[6] This clear difference in practice and context begs the

[4]Interview of associational leader by Amaney Jamal, summer 1999.

[5]Piatonni, *Clientelism, Interests, and Democratic Representation,* 3. Clientelism and corruption do exist in democracies; however, according to Simona Piatonni, "[e]xisting democracies strike different compromises between the protection of particular interests and the promotion of the general interest, hence represent different mixes of particularism and universalism."

[6]Schlumberger, "The Arab Middle East and the Question of Democratization"; Ismael, *Middle East Politics Today,* 74; Bellin, "Contingent Democrats," 175; and Bellin, "The Robustness of Authoritarianism in the Middle East."

question of whether civic associations in the service of political reform can travel from the democratic West, where states are not embedded in societies as they are in the rest of the world. But in states where government extends into all facets of civil society, as is characteristic of many nondemocratic and state-centralized nations, governments intervene more directly in associational life; they promote specific agendas, fund certain programs, and monitor associational activities. Particularly in nondemocratic polarized polities (with strong pro-regime and anti-regime cleavages) like those in Palestine and other Arab countries, ruling governments extend their influence by promoting associational agendas that directly serve their political mandate to the detriment of the general interests of the polity and of basic democratic procedures.

Hence the question of this book is whether or how civic associations can promote democratic attitudes and behaviors useful for democratic governance. Despite their role in Western democracies, civic associations—regardless of whether they are church societies or sports clubs—reproduce elements of the political context in which they exist and structure themselves accordingly. Where associational contexts are dominated by patron-client tendencies, associations, too, become sites for the replication of those vertical ties.

By examining associational realities in the context of the West Bank during the height of the Oslo Peace Process (1993–99), this book offers key insights into the political conditions that promote or depress "democratizing associationalism." The book also extends its findings to Morocco, Egypt, and Jordan, arguing that the relationship of associations to clientelistic and authoritarian governments is dramatically different from that between associations and democracies. In authoritarian contexts, associational life cannot be expected to yield the types of democratic values and outcomes associated with associationalism in Western democracies. In particular, this book examines the relationship between associational life in the West Bank and levels of civic engagement among the Palestinian citizenry. But before we address this issue, it is worth examining the argument championing civic associations in the democratic West, especially in the United States, more closely.

## ASSOCIATIONS IN WESTERN DEMOCRATIC CONTEXTS

It is difficult to argue with the proposition that civic associations—the YMCA, the Elks Club, church clubs, bowling leagues, trade unions, and so on—form the bedrock of modern Western democracies. The habits of association foster patterns of civility important for successful democracies.[7]

[7]Tocqueville, *Democracy in America.*

Civic organizations serve as agents of democratic socialization. In *Democracy in America,* Alexis de Tocqueville attributes the success of American democracy to its rich associational life. Associations serve as "schools for civic virtue." "Nothing," Tocqueville asserts, "is more deserving of our attention than the intellectual and moral associations of America. . . . [In associations,] feelings and opinions are recruited, the heart is enlarged, and the human mind is developed, only by the reciprocal influence of men upon each other."[8] Scholars who follow Tocqueville posit that citizens who participate in civic organizations are more likely to learn the importance of tolerance, pluralism, and respect for the law. Associational members not only learn that they have a right to be represented by their governments, but they also learn more about their potential political roles in society.[9]

The argument that higher levels of civic engagement are a product of associational life is the cornerstone of most contemporary literature on civil society. Active civic participation and engagement are necessary to sustain competent, responsive, and effective democratic institutions. Larry Diamond argues that "a rich associational life supplements the role of political parties in stimulating participation [and] increasing the political efficacy and skill of democratic citizens."[10] Hence, in democracies, especially Western ones, associational life helps instill values and practices essential to democratic governance.

Associational life also seems to increase the levels of social capital (networks and interpersonal trust) among members. In *Making Democracy Work,* Robert Putnam argues that trust and norms of reciprocity increase within organizations, thereby augmenting the likelihood of cooperative ventures among members of society as a whole. This increase in social capital in turn encourages people to "stand up to city hall" or engage in other forms of behavior that provide an incentive for better government performance. In Putnam's formulation, the density of horizontal voluntary associations among citizens (in contrast to the vertical associations under the dominion of the state) correlates with strong and effective local government: "strong society; strong state."[11]

Associations also foster democracy by mobilizing ordinary citizens in the political process. They and other civic networks can serve as political catalysts, bringing constituents into mainstream politics. The competition among these organized groups in the public arena results in public policy initiatives. In this view, associations are critical in a representative democracy. They funnel constituency preferences to mainstream policy

---

[8]Ibid., 200–201.
[9]Diamond and Plattner, "Toward Democratic Consolidation," 232–33.
[10]Ibid., 232–33.
[11]Putnam, *Making Democracy Work,* 176.

debates.[12] Civic organizations also reduce the costs of collective action by serving as collectivizing forums that bring citizens together.

Finally, civic organizations with substantial memberships can place the necessary constraints on authoritarian impulses within the government. Civic organizations serve as key sites for political mobilization, recruitment, and expression, working as counterweights to centralized governing apparatuses and encouraging sectors of society to oppose authoritarian tendencies. Associational life is particularly important in helping to hold states accountable, pressuring them to make more democratic concessions and checking the powers of authoritarian leaders. In Eastern Europe and the former Soviet Union, for instance, civic organizations contributed to the downfall of communist regimes.[13] This idea has been at the center of much of the literature on mobilization, opposition-regime relations, social movements, and revolutions.

The relationships between associational life and democratic outcomes reveal an underlying theme: a convergence of changes in attitude among individuals at the association level and increasing political participation within society as a whole, both of which are supportive of democratic outcomes. Associational members with higher levels of social capital exhibit a "self-interest that is alive to the interests of others" and therefore tend to care more about local community affairs. This in turn drives associational members to express their concerns through appropriate political channels.[14] Active association members with high social capital are also more likely to cooperate with others in ways that support democracy. When local concerns arise, members are more likely to take their complaints to local government officials rather than develop clientelistic ties. When attitudes and behaviors converge through active civic participation, democratic institutions become more effective.

Associational life, the argument goes, not only promotes and consolidates democracies but also makes democratic institutions stronger and more effective. But little attention has been paid to the fact that most of the research linking associational life to broader and more effective forms of civic engagement relies on evidence from democratic, mostly Western states, where autonomous interest groups already exist and are able to influence government in bottom-up fashion.[15] These studies conclude that,

---

[12] Huckfeldt, Plutzer, and Sprague, "Alternative Contexts of Political Behavior"; Rosenstone and Hansen, *Mobilization, Participation, and Democracy;* and Verba, Nie, and Kim, *Participation and Political Equality.*

[13] Huntington, *The Third Wave;* Przeworski, *Democracy and the Market;* and Evans, "The Eclipse of the State?"

[14] Putnam, *Making Democracy Work,* 88.

[15] Seminal works in this vein include Putnam, *Making Democracy Work;* and Verba, Schlozman, and Brady, *Voice and Equality.*

in democracies, associational life is important in enhancing the generation of specific qualities important for democratic citizenship, such as political efficacy, interpersonal trust, moderation, and support for democratic institutions and forms of political participation. The assumption that democratic institutions and autonomous interest groups *already exist* is embedded in the causal mechanisms linking individuals, at the associational level, to broader and more collective forms of participation that support institutional democratic outcomes. But how could higher levels of civic engagement lead to more conscientious voters if the right to vote freely, for example, is not already guaranteed?

The causal mechanisms that link associational members to broader forms of political participation within democracies depend on the availability of democratic participatory institutions. The posited relationship between civic associations and democracy is a circular and self-reinforcing relationship. Democratic socialization, the promotion of social capital that enables broader forms of democratic participation, and the mobilization of interests through democratic channels are all based on an unexamined norm of democracy: associations will promote the attitudes and behaviors important for members to make use of *existing* democratic political institutions.[16] Higher levels of civic engagement and more effective democratic governance, therefore, shape and reinforce one another in an endogenous relationship. Democratic institutions shape the way associations link their members to broader forms of political participation. Associations also instill attitudes and behaviors supportive of the available democratic structures in society.

The Tocquevillean strand of the literature on democracy and civic engagement focuses on what happens within associations. The acts of meeting, discussing, and debating generate qualities and predispositions compatible with democratic citizenship. That the internal dynamics of associations alone may create qualities that bode well for democratic citizenship is compelling, especially if these very qualities are reinforced and supported beyond the confines of associations. What happens outside an organization, however, is as important as what happens within. This means that exporting the idea of participation in civic associations to promote democracy in nondemocratic states is considerably more problematic.

In democratic societies, the merits of exercising one's rights democratically may reinforce habits of the heart that prefigure democracy. In nondemocratic societies, too, citizens may realize the importance of moderation, tolerance, and care for the local community. When the topics of

---

[16] The fourth claim, that associations can serve as counterweights to the state, is also applicable only in settings where civic sectors will not face harsh retaliation for advancing agendas that contradict or undermine the rule of the regime in power.

discussion within their associations also center on the nondemocratic context of the society at large, however—such as corruption among public officials, the lack of political recourse available to citizens, and the scarcity of general government service provisions—habits consistent with democratic citizenship may diminish. If members come to realize, through active civic participation, that the representation of particular interests through nondemocratic means is the norm and not the exception, that the government will promote and supply representation to only interests that correspond with its rule, and that those interested in general welfare polices can potentially be blocked from representation and participation, then the promotion and reinforcement of associational habits and predispositions should be dramatically different from those patterns which emerge in democracies.

Putnam has found that interpersonal trust is valuable for enhancing behavior that supports democratic rule. Higher levels of interpersonal trust also work to reinforce democratic rule, but they may be less applicable to nondemocratic societies. Indeed, in nondemocratic societies it is not clear how social capital can enhance the democratic governance of a regime. Social capital in democratic settings may create opportunities for citizens to collectively seek the help of democratic institutions and thus legitimate these democratic institutions. This may also be true in nondemocratic regions, where higher levels of social trust can enable citizens to seek out local public officials through any available avenue—whether formal (directly through the state) or informal (through clientelistic channels). Seeking the help of local public officials in this manner, however, similarly legitimizes authoritarian state behaviors and clientelistic channels. Just as associational life in northern Italy promotes civic engagement in ways that are important for the efficiency of northern Italy's local governance, so too does associational life in southern Italy promote civic engagement in ways that sustain the inefficiency of local governance in southern Italy. Does the lack of social capital in southern Italy promote ineffective democratic institutions? Or do ineffective democratic institutions promote levels of civic engagement, including social capital, supportive of nondemocratic procedures and institutions? If the latter is true, I posit, then social capital can be important in the reinforcement of any government in power, regardless of whether it is democratic or nondemocratic.

In Western democracies, states are not embedded in their societies, and they differ from nondemocratic states in the Arab world (and elsewhere) in important and marked ways. Most notably, in Western democracies, autonomous interest groups already exist; channels of political participation are already guaranteed; and blatant clientelism, patronage, and corruption play a less important role in everyday political life than they do in the Arab world. What, then, is to be said about the role of associations in enhancing levels of civic engagement in nondemocratic settings, such as the West Bank, where existing political institutions do not support the types of civic participation associated with more effective democracy?

Open to question, then, is the premise that civic associations will promote democracy unequivocally and across the board. Putnam, for one, argues that "those concerned with democracy and development in the South [Italy] ... should be building a more civic community."[17] In Putnam's argument, such a community should result from a higher degree of associational participation. Implicit in this argument is the correspondence of higher levels of social capital with higher levels of support for democratic procedures and norms. Other scholars make the same point, with similar implications. Larry Diamond writes that "associational life can ... promot[e] an appreciation of the obligations as well as the rights of democratic citizens."[18] It is inconceivable, however, that Putnam meant to correlate higher levels of social capital with support for anti-democratic procedures and norms—indeed, with anything other than democratic institutions and procedures, if the goal is more effective democratic institutions.[19] Furthermore, the improvement of democratic governance through civic engagement depends on the existence of associational life within democratic contexts where political institutions are both available and responsive. Otherwise, how would interest in local affairs promote democratic outcomes in areas where the channels of expression or the ability to lobby local representatives are either limited or inaccessible? In such areas, higher levels of interest in community affairs do not necessarily correlate with broader forms of political behavior that advance democracy or shore up democratic norms. The means to do so in each context are simply too different.

Associations, in these formulations, serve as vehicles for citizen representation. In democratic states, where channels exist for voicing citizen concerns and where government institutions are responsive, attitudes about the importance of government as a representative body can be solidified within associations, especially where citizens seek governmental intervention for problems that may arise in their daily lives. Associations in nondemocratic regions can attempt to link citizens to states, but again, the ability to do so depends on existing political institutions that differ from those in democracies. On the one hand, if associations directly seek

---

[17]Putnam, *Making Democracy Work,* 185.

[18]Diamond and Plattner, "Toward Democratic Consolidation," 230–31.

[19]Fukuyama, "Social Capital, Civil Society, and Development," 11. As Fukuyama says, "[a]n abundant stock of social capital is presumably what produces a dense civil society, which in turn has been almost universally seen as a necessary condition for modern liberal democracy (in Ernest Gellner's phrase, 'no civil society, no democracy')."

government channels but find they do not have access to government offices or to clientelistic ties, they may develop attitudes about participation that do not conform to the anticipated generation of political attitudes in democratic states. They may instead become rebellious. Having been shut out of government institutions, these associations and their members may not seek government help. On the other hand, if the association has strong connections to government through clientelistic channels, members may learn that in order to derive benefits, resources, and responses from the government, they need to seek informal, clientelistic channels of representation. In these cases, associations can very capably reinforce clientelistic tendencies within a given polity and further muster support for clientelistic forms of participation.

The argument that civic associations can serve as monitors or counterweights to the state again depends on the context. Many states severely restrict freedom of association specifically to prevent associations from assuming watchdog roles. In democratic settings, the freedom granted associations invites a multiplicity of interests and views to enter the mainstream and support broader democratic policies and forms of participation. In nondemocratic settings, by contrast, an association's ability to operate freely often depends on its agenda and other programmatic activities. Those that have the potential to disrupt the status quo often find themselves facing restrictions on their operation—if they are not disbanded altogether. Conversely, associations supporting the nondemocratic regime in power enjoy rights and privileges not guaranteed to associations in opposition. What type of civic engagement, then, do these pro-government associations encourage? First, associations endorsing the current nondemocratic regime may promote values that are not critical of the regime's policies; second, they can also reinforce clientelistic behavior. Both possibilities are at odds with studies finding that associational life promotes democratic citizenship and effective democratic institutions.

The overall political context in which associations operate, I argue, shapes the ways in which associations may or may not produce democratic change. Too often, associations that house civil society are credited with heroic accomplishments without specific attention being paid to the ways that preexisting state-society relations mediate associational activities and patterns of operation.[20] For example, in institutions where the survivability of associations is linked to regime endorsement, then the

---

[20]For discussions on the ways in which civic associations may operate against democracy, see Berman, "Civil Society and the Collapse of the Weimar Republic," 401; Fung, "Associations and Democracy"; Dylan Riley, "Civic Association and Authoritarian Regimes in Interwar Europe: Italy and Spain in Comparative Perspective," *American Sociological Review* (2005).

political regime—whether democratic or nondemocratic—will find civil society beneficial. In many parts of the globe, civil society can and does reinforce existing political regimes and not democracy per se.

Because political institutions shape civic engagement and civic attitudes, both the content and the form of civic engagement will differ across varying political contexts. People engage their surroundings, which in turn shape attitudes and beliefs about civic participation. And although higher levels of civic engagement in democratic frameworks may lead to patterns of participation conducive to or supportive of democracy, in nondemocratic settings higher levels of civic engagement may not necessarily lead to similar trajectories of participation. Thus, the absence of accessible channels of political participation will not only hinder some forms of participation but also shape one's attitudes and beliefs about participation. Individuals will develop opinions, attitudes, norms, and perceptions influenced directly by the political context in which they operate. Since patterns of political participation differ in nondemocratic settings, patterns of civic engagement should differ as well. Even within similar contexts, variation will exist among members' civic engagement according to associational interactions with the political world around them.

## ASSOCIATIONAL LIFE IN PALESTINE

Palestine is a particularly rich area in which to examine the effectiveness of civic membership on democratization. After nearly thirty years of living under Israeli Occupation, and after eight years of the first Intifada,[21] Palestinians began experiencing a new relationship to their governing apparatus, the Palestinian National Authority (PNA). Although most Palestinians in 1999 were living under the direct rule of the PNA, the Israeli Occupation persisted in the majority of lands on the West Bank. By 1999, the majority of Palestinians had been living under the rule of the PNA for nearly six years. Had the Israeli Occupation ended and a peaceful agreement been reached, Palestinians would have been on the road to building a state.[22] Studying associational life in Palestine, therefore, offers

---

[21]The first Palestinian Uprising started in December 1987 and ended in 1993, with the signing of the Oslo peace accords between Israel and the Palestinians. The current Intifada II or Aqsa Intifada started in September of 2000 and ended after Arafat's death in November 2004. Please note that data were gathered for this project between 1998 and 1999.

[22]Some might argue that the Palestinian case is not an appropriate one for this study, because the Palestinians lack a state. I disagree. My examination of associational effects on attitudes and behaviors of members assesses attitudes about the "government" in power and not the "state." Max Weber's criteria for a constituted political community require that the government rule in a territory and possess the physical force requisite to dominate that

us an examination of the ways in which civil society can plausibly influence democratic and state-building processes.

In 1999, the PNA, though ostensibly democratic, in truth mirrored much of the rest of the Arab world. It was a classic authoritarian regime that reinforced the centrality of the government through a network that included both formal and informal patron-client relationships. The increasing authoritarianism of the PNA left supporters and opponents at odds and thus resulted in a growing polarization at the societal levels between these two sectors. Supporters were right to point out that Arafat had very little choice but to centralize his power. Arafat and the PNA were still dealing with the Israeli Occupation. In essence, the Oslo stipulations demanding security for Israelis at all costs meant that Arafat needed to consolidate his power immediately and turn a blind eye to human rights abuses when collective punishments were enforced. This, of course, did not impress the Palestinian people, but significant sectors of the population were willing to give Arafat's PNA a chance. After all, Arafat's PNA controlled only 17% of the West Bank. Not only did the Israeli Occupation persist, however, but it became painfully clear that Israel was single-handedly determining the parameters of a future Palestinian state: one that would be divided and segregated with bypass roads and new Israeli settlement projects. Arafat was in a bind. On the one hand, he wanted to deliver a Palestinian state. In return however, Arafat was getting very little. The Palestinian state seemed all the more elusive. Unable to deal with growing Palestinian frustration, Arafat began curbing and limiting the channels available to these oppositional elements. Furthermore, Arafat was able to build a very elaborate, overinflated bureaucracy. Critics pointed out that this was a pattern all too paramount in the Arab world. Arab states have managed authoritarian consolidation through state patronage for decades. In response, supporters pointed out that Arafat was only helping, by providing much-needed jobs to the Palestinian people. With Israeli closures on the West Bank and Gaza, jobs were needed. And finally, supporters of Arafat claimed that opponents were chipping away at Arafat's credibility in the face of very difficult negotiations with Israel and the United States. It was bad enough that the United States and Israel consistently blamed Arafat when anything went wrong; he did not need Palestinians to endorse the biased patterns of the Israelis and the Americans. Therefore, what emerged in Palestine under Arafat's PNA was a highly centralized regime, where Arafat rewarded followers and sanctioned defectors. He was able to do

---

territory. The PNA also possessed key characteristics of power in a political community, namely, a monopoly of the legitimate use of force and implementation of the legal order. See Weber, *Economy and Society*.

so because he skillfully instituted a system of clientelism and patronage that permeated society.

In 1998 and 1999, I set out to better understand the nature of state-society relations in Palestine. Because my focus is on state-society relations, this book offers a glimpse of civil society in 1998–99 that juxtaposes Palestinian civil society with the governing PNA (and *not* the Israeli Occupation). By focusing on this dimension of regime–civil society relations, I am not attempting to downplay the overarching and pervasive role the Israeli Occupation plays in the everyday lives of ordinary Palestinian citizens. Rather, the purpose of this book is to explore the ways in which regime (PNA) and civil society interactions shaped patterns of civic engagment more broadly during the Oslo period (1993–2000).

In focusing on the nature of PNA–civil society relations in Palestine, I feel that it is imperative to clarify that the PNA, while not a state, was very much a governing authority. The Israeli Occupation however remained crucial in shaping the ways in which civil society interacted with the PNA. In order to contextualize the Palestinian case carefully, the Israeli Occupation will be present in much of the analysis in this book. However, this book is not about the relationship between Palestinian civil society and the Israeli Occupation. Although this is a topic of great importance and significance, the terrain of this book is limited to the relations between Palestinian civil society and the PNA. Throughout the book, I reference the ways the existing and ongoing Israeli Occupation shaped Palestinian regime-society relations, but I do not discuss, in depth, the overall implications of the Israeli Occupation on Palestinian civil society.

My goal is to understand the democratic effects of associational life in contexts where existing regimes are embedded in societies. Therefore, I focus on the relationships between the authoritarian PNA and Palestinian civil society. The type of regime–civil society relations I discuss here are not limited to the context of the Palestinian case. And although the Israeli Occupation, many will argue, served Arafat's attempts to consolidate authority, similar external threats have served the same purpose in other Arab states. Pan-Arab nationalist countries have used the logic of external threats to further consolidate regime rules. Even today, while democracy promotion initiatives garner much applause and enthusiasm, these initiatives also give governing structures more legitimacy to build security measures (against politicized sectors) that often require further regime centralization and consolidation. Therefore, the implications of my book travel beyond the Palestinian context and apply to state-society relations in other Arab countries as well. I demonstrate that parallels exist between the Palestinian case and those of Morocco, Jordan, and Egypt. Whether existing efforts to promote democracy in the Arab world, including Palestine, succeed has yet to be determined. In the interim, this book offers a glimpse at the role civil societies can possibly play in these transitions, given the existing conditions on the ground in the Arab world.

## THE ASSOCIATIONAL PUZZLE

Associational life continued to flourish during the Oslo period. During the 1980s the strategies of political mobilization employed by local Palestinian elites dramatically expanded associational life in the West Bank. In the 1990s international donor assistance contributed to the growth of the voluntary sector as well. Although participation in these associations had enlivened civic engagement and increased levels of interpersonal trust (a measure of social capital), the relationships between these main dimensions of civic engagement (political knowledge, civic involvement, and community engagement), interpersonal trust,[23] and support for democratic institutions *were not directly related to one another.* Using data from two surveys, one from the general Palestinian population and the other from association members and in-depth qualitative interviews with over sixty association leaders, I found that patterns of civic engagement, political knowledge, community engagement, civic involvement, and support for democratic institutions were inversely related to levels of interpersonal trust. Contrary to the expectations of existing theories derived from Western democratic settings, these findings pose an important empirical question. What explains this divergence in civic engagement indicators among Palestinian association members?

The answer this book puts forward lies in the nature of state-society relations. In centralized clientelistic settings, associations that support the regime will exhibit higher levels of interpersonal trust and lower degrees of democratic forms of civic engagement. Conversely, associations not linked to the regime will hold lower levels of interpersonal trust and higher levels of democratic civic engagement. The results here provide a counternarrative of the civic processes and pathways that instill, reinforce, and promote specific attitudes at the expense of others. In semidemocratic or authoritarian states, these aspects of "civic culture" do not, in fact, correlate with one another. In the West Bank, these attitudes and behaviors are not linked. This chapter aims to make further sense of the sources that underlie this inverse relationship in dem-

---

[23]In this study, I employ the phrase *interpersonal trust* to denote trust in others as well a sense of responsibility toward others in society.

ocratic indicators among associational members in the West Bank and in authoritarian states more broadly. Using the existing literature as a conceptual guide, I offer a more particularized explanation of these determinants and the plausible outcomes of the existing relationships among these indicators.

Briefly, in polities with strong patron-client relationships that function under state influence, associational life mediates levels of interpersonal trust, civic engagement, and support for democratic institutions differently. The polarization (and further segmentation) of the Palestinian political polity into pro- and anti-PNA factions determines the impact of civic life on civic attitudes. Levels of interpersonal trust are higher among members of pro-PNA associations, while support for the PNA inversely correlates with levels of support for democratic institutions. Further, support for democratic institutions strongly correlates with higher levels of civic engagement.

## CLIENTELISM AND PATRONAGE

The existence of clientelism today "defies the modern notion of representation, where all citizens should be guaranteed equal political access" by mere virtue of citizenship.[24] Instead, clientelism provides clients with paths to exclusive services and influence in return for their support of their patron. It subverts the democratic process: the client who receives money to vote in a certain way; the individual who is granted political access because he supports the party in power; the woman who pays lip service to the state in return for benefits—the list is endless.[25] The PNA was rife with such relationships, which take the form of a pyramid-shaped clientelistic network characteristic of strong, one-party states. The major beneficiaries of clientelism in these states are regime affiliates. (The second arrangement is what I will call the diffused clientelistic model, and it relies on a less centralized government apparatus. In this latter model, clientelism permeates virtually all social arenas. Electoral clientelism, factional clientelism, and business clientelism are examples of scattered clientelistic networks.[26] Power relations in these settings are distributed among numerous leaders. In the diffused clientelistic network, there is no one centralized nucleus of authority that controls political access.) In the

---

[24] Roniger and Gunes-Ataya, *Democracy, Clientelism, and Civil Society*, 9.

[25] Ibid., 9; Fox, "The Difficult Transition from Clientelism to Citizenship: Lessons from Mexico," 151; Kitschelt, "Linkages between Citizens and Politicians."

[26] Craig, "Caste, Class, and Clientelism." See, for example, India.

pyramid model, the state is the premier patron, and secondary and tertiary patrons are directly linked back to the state.[27]

The impact of state clientelism in state-centralized regimes (those that extend to all domains of civil society) on the democratic effects of associational life is multidimensional. The parameters of this political context constrain associational life at many junctures. Primarily, state-sponsored associations receive immediate political access and benefits not accorded to nonstate associations. Clientelistic networks further reinforce vertical linkages between state leaders and citizens, at the expense of horizontal linkages among associations. This dual effect of centralized clientelism structures the ways in which associations interact with their political environment and with one another. Where associations derive resources and benefits from the state, they are more likely to endorse government initiatives—even if those initiatives are nondemocratic. Further, because associations are linked to the state, they rely less on one another.

As a conceptual term, *clientelism* has come to encompass the various relationships between individuals and power brokers at either end of vertical and hierarchical networks. Clientelism is about mutual trust and reciprocity, beneficial to both client and patron, and it is a worldwide phenomenon. While it is prevalent in the nondemocratic world, it is not foreign to democratic countries, several of which—including Brazil, Mexico, South Korea, and India—exhibit considerable levels of clientelism.[28] In fact, client-patron relations are quite common among parties and constituencies in more developed democracies as well.[29]

Although some alternate forms may exist across political contexts, the way clientelism structures state-society relations depends on the locus of power from which it emerges. The power structure underlying clientelistic relations in return determines the degree of a client's autonomy. In more democratically diffuse clientelistic settings, clients possess more autonomy because they have more patrons to choose from. In state-centralized clientelistic settings, the narrow clientelistic superbroker—the state—limits clientelistic options and thus reduces the autonomy of

---

[27] For discussion of the importance of centralization for clientelistic linkages between citizens and states, see Powell, "Peasant Society and Clientelistic Politics"; Kohli, "Centralization and Powerlessness"; and Hagopian, "Traditional Politics." This definition largely incorporates Jonathan Fox's definition of authoritarian clientelism in "The Difficult Transition from Clientelism to Citizenship: Lessons from Mexico." His definition captures clientelistic relations "where imbalanced bargaining relations require the political subordination of clients and are reinforced by the the threat of coercion." My definition extends beyond that of Fox to encompass the centralized nature of authoritarian clientelistic regimes characteristic of many Arab states. Similar patterns are found in India's rule under the Congress Party in the 1950s and in Brazil under Arena until the mid-1970s.

[28] USAID report.

[29] Kitschelt, "Linkages between Citizens and Politicians."

clients. The autonomy of actors—or in this case, civic associations—depends on the overall political regime. Hence, in state-centralized regimes, where clientelism serves to replicate and extend the power of the state, civic associations enjoy less autonomy than civic associations in more established democratic settings.

State-centralized clientelism is characteristic of many states in the Arab world, and not just in the West Bank. Many regimes encourage "the formation of a limited number of officially recognized, non-competing, state-supervised groups," extending government influence to all facets of society.[30] Arab countries tend to fit this category of states that exhibit both control over and support for civic organizations. "It is textbook knowledge and hardly contested that Arab socio-political systems are characterized by strongly neo-patrimonial political rule and thus by asymmetric relation of superiority and subordination," argues Oliver Schlumberger. "This is paralleled in society at large by networks of patronage and clientelism that pervade not only the political realm but societies as a whole." States across the Middle East are so deeply embedded in clientelistic relations that, as Schlumberger goes on to argue, Arab civil societies are "in no position to impose reforms or even exert pressure to an extent beyond the control of the state."[31]

Centralization is possible because of the coercive, centralized capacity of the state.[32] Atul Kohli argues that "when the polity is organized as a democracy coercion definitely cannot be the main currency that leaders utilize to influence socioeconomic change."[33] In the Arab world the state is not held accountable, because there are very few mechanisms through which non-regime-supporting associations can do so. Opposition is swiftly quelled or defeated. In these formulations Arab societies are either in government-supporting networks or they are not. Ismael argues, "Throughout the region, states attempted to impose hegemony over civil society through oppressive and coercive measures administered through juridical, administrative, or security channels. In regimes that oppress and persecute political opposition, there is little room for autonomy."[34] Without autonomy, there can be little room for viable and competitive civil organizations outside government networks. Organizations outside state-

[30]Anoushiravan and Murphy, "Transformation of the Corporatist State."

[31]Schlumberger, "The Arab Middle East and the Question of Democratization," 114, 117; and Hamzeh, "Clientelism, Lebanon."

[32]Bellin, "The Robustness of Authoritarianism in the Middle East." According to Tareq Ismal, "Of the nineteen states in the Middle East, only eleven are signatories of the United Nations convention against torture, and most of those who are signatory have expressed strong reservations with Articles 21 and 22, which require the state in question to submit to examination whenever grievance petitions are filled."

[33]Bellin, "The Robustness of Authoritarianism in the Middle East."

[34]Ismael, *Middle East Politics Today,* 74.

centralized relations are economically deprived and cannot depend on formal institutions to represent their interests. Because these associations exist in centralized authoritarian settings, their ability to produce change is next to impossible.

Further, state centralization and the lack of democratic accountability cultivate corrupt, rent-seeking behavior among public officials. One study of Morocco finds that regime corruption suits only the longevity of the state, and resources are devoted to patronage and diverted from other useful purposes such as productive investment strategies.[35] While patron-client relations need not be corrupt, a sentiment echoed in clientelistic studies in Western democratic settings,[36] "patronage and corruption overlap" in Morocco. All this has clear implications for the role of civic associations in the Arab world.

In the absence of viable democratic institutions that separate and decentralize authority, the same patterns of civic engagement that pave the way to more effective democratic institutions in already democratic settings may generate attitudes and behaviors in settings like that of the West Bank that either reinforce the prevailing political status quo or distance citizens from the regime in power. Furthermore, where centralized governing institutions, clientelistic ties, and local corruption restrict associational life, civic associations—depending on their relationship to their immediate political surroundings—will shape patterns of civic engagement that reflect an association's position within its political context. Thus, in some cases associational life may produce dimensions of democratic citizenship, such as support for democratic institutions; however, in other cases it may produce dimensions of engagement that support authoritarian rule, specifically that of the ruling authoritarian government. I argue that the way organizations orchestrate and negotiate relationships with the political institutions around them influences the way organizations affect patterns of civic engagement, interpersonal trust, and support for democratic institutions among their members.

The existence of patron-client relations between the PNA and Palestinian society reinforces the polarized and politicized context of the West Bank. Both associational clients and nonclients are affected by their political context, albeit in different ways. Clientelistic associations vertically link their members to the larger political environment. Absent a clientelistic linkage to the PNA, the leaders and members of these associations work among themselves to fulfill their associational goals. These nonclientelistic associations are more horizontally organized. Leaders depend on their members, and they do not see themselves as key links

[35]Waterbury, "Endemic and Planned Corruption," 537, 555, as cited by Hutchcroft, "The Politics of Privilege."

[36]See, for example, Kitschelt, "Linkages between Citizens and Politicians."

between government and member constituencies. Because these associations do not enjoy the benefits of government privilege, they find it expensive and dangerous to expand their horizontal networks to other like-minded associations. Although horizontally structured, these associations remain marginalized.

Patron-client relations, however, allow for vertical ties within the organizational schema of associations. Among those associations that have close ties to the ruling government in power, vertically structured relations ensue. Because clientelistic leaders have close ties to government, they can deliver services and favors directly to their members, who become increasingly dependent on their leaders.

The type of relationship that the leaders have with existing political structures acts as a template framing the attitudes and behaviors of associational members. Where leaders enjoy special status because of strong ties to government, members, too, derive resources and benefits that reinforce the image of a benevolent PNA. By contrast, leaders who are critical of or in opposition to the PNA will reinforce member attitudes and behaviors that are similarly critical of the government. Supporters and critics of the PNA will therefore structure the civic engagement of their members differently. On the one hand, those who are supporters—who are part of the PNA "in crowd"—reveal to their members the tremendous opportunities associated with the PNA. The message to members is one that motivates involvement in PNA institutions in order to reap the benefits and rewards of loyal participation. On the other hand, critics will urge their members to be skeptical and cautious in their relationships with PNA institutions and discourage members from approaching these "corrupt" institutions. This is the case that led to Hamas's electoral victory in the 2006 Palestinian Legislative Council elections. Hamas, during the Oslo period, remained skeptical of the PNA and for the most part refused clientelistic ties to the PNA while it continued to mobilize its constituents at the civil society level.

When deciding to allocate voluntarily one's capital for the common good of the community in the West Bank, it becomes readily apparent that involvement in pro-PNA associations offers better benefits and perquisites than involvement in non-PNA-supporting associations. Because pro-PNA associations are in close vertical proximity to the governing institution, they can deliver more of the material benefits potentially supplied by those associations. As a result, one tends to see a greater number of pro-PNA civic associations. In settings where citizens depend on associations for basic services like food and shelter, dependency on associations increases. Members who choose not to join pro-PNA associations sometimes do so on the basis of strong ideological, if not factional, grounds.

It is not surprising, then, that in 1999 pro-PNA groups dominated the associational terrain in the West Bank. By partaking in associations that are supportive of the PNA, members feel that in some way they are not only aiding the national leadership but also adhering to—not necessarily "reinforcing"—a set of norms that is already established. Where associational leaders are already clients of the PNA, they appeal to their members' sensibilities on the grounds of aiding Palestinian society by supporting the leadership that is working toward larger national aspirations of liberation. Through supporting the nationalist project, these members reap pertinent benefits for their involvement. Conforming to the status quo makes these volunteers materially happier than those members who challenge the prevailing status quo. Those non-PNA members who look on as pro-PNA associations prosper are shocked, frustrated: they must struggle to offer meager programmatic initiatives, whereas pro-PNA associations seem to bask in clientelistic ease. They feel that their voluntary efforts are futile, for they continue to witness the manifestation of patron-client ties in Palestinian society.

The nature of clientelism in the Arab world today is particular to this historical juncture. Although during the height of Oslo, Palestine was less authoritarian and repressive than other Arab countries, with the onset of the PNA similar patterns of state-centralized clientelism began to take root and permeate state-society relations. A more detailed discussion of the political context is provided in chapter 2, which offers a detailed historical analysis of the emergence and evolution of associational life in the West Bank. There, I illustrate the underpinnings of the political context polarized between PNA-supporting and non-PNA-supporting associations.

Based on ethnographic interviews conducted with associational leaders in 1999, chapter 3 captures the multidimensionality of this polarization. Attitudes about the PNA extend beyond resource maximization and immediate material benefits. Ideological inclinations that encompass nationalistic sentiments, convictions about social justice that address such issues as the alleviation of poverty, and firm principles about democratic citizenship all play salient roles in associational identification with the government in power. And although associational life is related to higher forms of civic engagement, the various indicators of civic engagement do not correspond to one another.

Chapter 4 breaks down associational types by carefully examining leadership roles and government affiliations in associations. Using survey data collected from association members and a national survey of Palestinians administered by the Jerusalem Media Communications Center in Jerusalem, this chapter tests the overall hypothesis of my study that linkages to existing political institutions mediate civic engagement. The weakness of the rule of law in the West Bank has resulted in nonresponsive governing institutions; in the absence of responsive governing institutions, local elites promote clientelism to play an important role in responding to citizen demands and needs. Leaders, therefore, can either connect their members to existing political institutions or further distance their members from political and public spaces altogether. This location of members vis-à-vis their immediate political surroundings directly influences the consistency of civic engagement.

Chapter 5 extends the findings of the detailed case study of the West Bank to Morocco and then offers a glimpse of associational life in Egypt and Jordan. Using World Values Survey data, this chapter offers evidence that supports my overall conclusion that not all associations are beneficial to democracy: associations more supportive of governing, nondemocratic institutions cultivate patterns of civic engagement different from those cultivated by less supportive associations. Civic engagement in and of itself need not be associated with positive democratic externalities. Subjecting levels of civic engagement to an analysis of the role that political realities play in shaping such engagement provides us with a more nuanced and accurate assessment as to when attitudes and behaviors normally seen as useful for democratic promotion in democratic settings are also beneficial for democratic outcomes in less democratic settings.

Chapter 6 examines the role of civic engagement, interpersonal trust, and support for democratic institutions among association members in the context of the West Bank. Interpersonal trust is in fact related to effective democratic outcomes, although its usefulness in state-centralized settings is less clear. By mapping social trust onto other forms of civic attitudes deemed important for democratic citizenship, this chapter seeks to offer new insights on how and when social capital aids democratic outcomes.

Civic associations, regardless of whether they are church societies or sports clubs, will reproduce elements of the political context in which they exist and will structure themselves accordingly. Where associational contexts are dominated by state-centralized, patron-client tendencies, then associations, too, become sites for the potential replication of those vertical ties. Belonging to a vertical associational context does not necessarily require that members "actively" choose to reinforce "hierarchical" and less "democratic" relations within their organizing communities. Rather, it signifies the ways in which available opportunities shape citizen choices about civic participation.

# CHAPTER TWO

# Associational Life in the Centralized Authoritarian Context of the West Bank

THE POLITICAL REALITIES that shape the output of associational life differ from neighborhood to neighborhood, state to state, and country to country. The next two chapters provide, through a detailed examination of political-associational interactions in the West Bank in 1999, a portable theoretical framework outlining the effects of associational life on the quality of civic engagement. Civic associations in the West Bank were polarized along two main axes—associations with close ties to and favorable opinions of the government (the PNA) and associations that more or less opposed the PNA.

Basic requirements of associational activity are necessary for active civic participation; that is, associations must perform in certain ways to ensure that their members are actively involved in activities and programs. Associations should ensure that their members meet, participate, and contribute to as well as actively engage in various programs. Aside from influencing members, associations are also directly influenced by their political context. In state-centralized clientelistic regimes, peppered with ineffective governing institutions, the rule of law is weak, and clientelism, corruption, and patrimony dominate state-society relations. Associations' political disposition and ideological relationship to local governing institutions determine their interactions with existing political institutions. In turn, this interaction shapes the consistency of associational life and its impact on civic engagement.

Since the emergence of the Palestinian National Authority in 1993, clientelism and patronage have defined state-society relations in the West Bank. Civic associations, too, have had to define—and in many cases, redefine—their relations to the government in power. Those associations with strong ties to the PNA derived more resources and benefits, security and prestige, legitimacy and credibility than associations without ties of similar strength. Associations in the good graces of the government received high media exposure and public visits from government officials; additionally, they were seldom harassed. Clientelism, patronage, and corruption have been common features across the developing world. In state-centralized settings, states opt to consolidate and centralize authority, rather than diffuse power through democratic institutions. The PNA's ability to establish a bona fide, classical, and expansive patron-client regime from the outset of its administration was due to the direct historical legacy of the Palestine Liberation Organization's (PLO) role in Palestinian political and civic life. This politicization of Palestinian civil society explained the polarization that emerged between PNA-supporting and nonsupporting civic associations. Further, this polarization determined the inconsistencies in patterns of civic engagement among Palestinian association members.

## The Failure of Oslo, PNA Corruption, and Democracy

On November 11, 2004, Yasir Arafat passed away. His dream, a goal of Palestinian struggle toward independence, remained unrealized. Palestinians across the board, supporters and opponents alike, mourned his passing. He left behind him an uncertain Palestinian future. Four years of the second Intifada had left any new Palestinian state infrastructure in shambles. The reoccupation of Palestinian-controlled areas by Israel had led to a horrific path of destruction. PNA buildings, police stations, and Palestinian records of the past decade were all but destroyed. The world came to see Arafat as an embattled leader locked up in his Muqat'a residence. The United States and Israel declared him forever a terrorist. Isolated and marginalized, Arafat still led the Palestinian people, and the Palestinian people still saw in him their national aspirations. In more ways than one, Arafat epitomized the Palestinian national struggle.

A major point of analysis in this chapter draws attention to levels of corruption within the ranks of the Palestinian National Authority in 1999. By 2004 many observers and skeptics were linking the demise of Oslo to levels of PNA corruption. It is important to note here, however, that the demise of Oslo cannot be attributed solely to corruption in the ranks of the PNA. It is also important to note that the lack of Palestinian democracy did not destroy Oslo. And certainly the lack of democracy in neighboring Egypt and Jordan did not prevent the signing of binding and durable peace agreements with Israel, either.

Yet, the painfully clear abuses of power diminished Palestinian support for the peace process, as did the existing realities of continued Israeli Occupation on the ground. By the end of 1999, it had become evident that the Palestinian vision of an independent state on the West Bank and in Gaza was completely at odds with the Israeli vision. The Israelis insisted on expanding settlements in the West Bank, continued to confiscate more West Bank territory in order to build roads to link these settlements to Israel, and completely disregarded the fact that these settlements were severely dividing the West Bank into incongruent, disconnected enclaves that in the end would allow little economic and political viability for the future Palestinian state. This fueled Palestinian resentment against Oslo, and it played brilliantly into the hands of Palestinian extremists. The more Israel demanded Arafat do something about them, the more they became invested in discrediting Arafat with continued violence.

When it became clear that Arafat was useless to Oslo, as he was able neither to control those against Oslo nor to keep his supporters on board, Israel and the United States demanded that he be replaced.[1] Therefore, the US demands for removing Arafat from power had more to do with finding a leader who would control the Palestinian people rather than promoting democracy for democracy's sake. Arafat was supposed to deliver peace and calm in return for whatever Israel was willing to offer him. That the Israeli conditions were not acceptable to the general Palestinian population seemed irrelevant. Arafat was believed to be able to manipulate and control the entire Palestinian population.[2] In the end, then, a miscalculation was made. Arafat was unable to destroy a Palestinian civic and political society whose very essence demanded independence and territorial integrity on the West Bank and in Gaza. Even as support for Oslo dissipated, the vast majority of Palestinians still supported a two-state solution.

.  .  .

During the seven years of the Oslo peace accords, Palestinians attempted to consolidate their institutions and build the foundations of a democratic state. Although the Israeli Occupation persisted, Palestinians were convinced that the Oslo Accords would result in a mutually acceptable two-state solution. With what little territorial control they had, Palestinians eagerly worked toward a democratic state. Quickly, however, Arafat began to consolidate his rule in ways that Palestinians found alarming. Would the future Palestinian state become "another" Arab authoritarian government? Was this consolidation necessary only to appease growing US and Israeli demands to counter Hamas? Or was Arafat simply being sympathetic to growing unemployment and providing much-needed jobs? The reasons why Arafat turned to authoritarianism are numerous and range from his personalistic style to broader strategic necessities. Arafat supporters were more sympathetic to his plight—negotiations with Israel were producing very few territorial concessions for the future Palestinian state. These supporters were willing to give Arafat the benefit

[1]Shikaki, "The Future of Palestine."
[2]Hammami and Tamari, "The Second Intifada."

of the doubt. Opponents were more skeptical and believed that Arafat was skillfully and deliberately creating another authoritarian regime. Regardless of the reasons behind Arafat's governing style, by 1999 the Palestinian National Authority was governing Palestinian society in an authoritarian way.

Institutionally, the West Bank had some democratic elements, such as popular election; however, because so much of the PNA was an extension of Arafat's personal rule, democratic institutions in the West Bank remained weak. My argument here calls for careful analysis of the manner in which institutional political realities in the West Bank directly structured the influence associations had on civic engagement. Like other citizens in the developing world, Palestinians lived in an environment with little democratic accountability, weak state institutions, limited access to government officials, and few channels—outside clientelistic networks—for citizen recourse. In the West Bank, under the auspices of the newly created PNA of 1994, the rule of law had yet to be implemented, the judiciary and the executive branches of government were still highly integrated, and a clear, coherent, and accessible system of arbitration remained in its nascent stages.

Within this type of environment, associations must carefully navigate the contours of existing political realities. Associations, that is, do not exist in a political vacuum. Although they are seen as plausible societal forces that may bring about statewide reforms, associations cannot exist without some form of recognition or approval from the state. In authoritarian states, associations that are considered threats to the state can easily be shut down.[3] Therefore, associations need to conform to basic, minimal state expectations if they are to even exist.[4] In state-centralized clientelistic settings, states extend their monopoly on power to the associational terrain.[5] Governments can provide services, rewards, and other carrots to associations that endorse the vision and programs of the state. In many corporatist states, government officials even encourage the creation of associations to further extend state influence into the realm of societal affairs.[6] States can also co-opt associational leaders, urging them to adopt more sympathetic and government-supporting stances. Pro-government associations have stronger ties to the government than non-supporting or neutral associations do, and they are therefore able to gain more public visibility. In states with government-controlled media, for

[3]Bratton and van de Walle, *Democratic Experiments in Africa.*

[4]Bermeo and Nord, "Civil Society after Democracy," 237–54. See ways in which state censorship and coercion stifle democratic connectedness between associations and larger representative democratic institutions.

[5]Chazen, "Engaging the State."

[6]Brynen, Korany, and Noble, "From Occupation to Uncertainty," 192–96; Bianchi, *Unruly Corporatism.*

instance, such associations can garner a great deal of media coverage.[7] Nonsupporting associations are at a great disadvantage, unable to promote their visions through viable channels of communication.[8] Supporters of the state are also able to command resources and benefits unattainable by non-government-supporting associations. In addition to resources that ensure their survival, associations in good standing with the government are able to access clientelistic channels and in some cases become clientelistic gateways themselves, thereby linking their members to the government. Blessed by the government, they are also offered a public platform through which to openly engage their members and the community at large; these close ties to the government facilitate the implementation of their programmatic initiatives. Within an authoritarian context, associations that have stronger ties to government are accorded privileges that non-government-supporting associations do not receive. This asymmetry influences the quality of civic engagement among associational members.

## POLITICAL CONTEXTUAL DIFFERENCE AND ASSOCIATIONAL LIFE

One might make the argument that pro-government associations in consolidated democratic settings are also accorded certain favors and privileges. This may be true, but the differences between the legal constraints on public officials in these democracies and state-centralized regimes are considerable. In democracies, consistent elections ensure the accountability of public officials to their constituents; this electoral risk also maintains government accountability to the public more broadly. As Susan Rose-Ackerman states, "the desire for re-election constrains the greed of politicians. The protection of civil liberties and free speech, which generally accompanies democratic electoral process, makes open and transparent government possible." In short, she continues, "the public can be an important check on the arbitrary exercise of power by government."[9] In consolidated democracies, furthermore, statutes control both corruption among public officials and government patronage. Pilar Domingo

---

[7]Amal Jamal, "State Building and Media Regime." In the West Bank, the PNA closed down several newspapers, including *al-Fajr* and *An al-Nahar,* for holding viewpoints oppositional to the PNA. Arafat had full control of the Palestinian Broadcasting Corporation and often made decisions about news content in the basement of his headquarters, where the television offices existed. Further, the PNA supervised the additional twenty cable stations that emerged.

[8]Carapico, "Foreign Aid," 391. Regarding Arab authoritarian states: "Governments monopolized the production and dissemination of information through ownership, censorship, licensure, national federations, and other mechanisms designed to limit independent political and intellectual activism."

[9]Rose-Ackerman, *Corruption and Government,* 113, 162.

has explored this aspect of democratic institutional checks in the Latin American context: "[t]raditionally," he writes, "the institutional design of legal accountability takes the form of various arrangements of separation of powers, on the one hand, and electoral control on the holders of public office, on the other hand."[10] Without an independent judiciary and an efficient system of arbitration, few mechanisms exist to hold authoritarian government leaders accountable. If government corruption is to be addressed, "[c]itizens must have a convenient means of lodging complaints and be protected against possible reprisals."[11] In many developing countries, however, including those in Latin America and the Middle East, the rule of law remains weak. Further, citizens tend to have very little faith in the judicial system: "[j]udicial systems reproduce an image of corruption, clientelism, and inefficiency and [are] not viewed as impartial administrators of justice or autonomous agents of constitutional and legal control."[12] Yet, although several states across the developing world suffer from ineffectual democratic institutions like those in many Latin American countries, they are not as centrally authoritarian as countries are in the Arab Middle East.

## THE POLARIZATION OF ASSOCIATIONAL LIFE IN THE WEST BANK: HISTORICAL OVERVIEW

In the West Bank, associational life in 1999 was extremely polarized; generally, associations were seen as either sympathetic or opposed to the PNA. Though this distinction may appear simplistic, such dichotomization contains a nuanced conglomeration of interests, allegiances, and ideologies that stem from a history of occupation, factionalism, elite realignment, and state- and nation-building initiatives. The categorization of associational life along these two main axes offers a political contextual framework through which to analyze the impact of associational life on civic engagement. It is these interactions that influence the quality and content of civic engagement among association members.

The Oslo Accords, signed in 1993, divided Palestinian history into two unique phases that explain not only the political situation under Oslo but also its impact on associational life. The West Bank and Gaza Strip fell under Israeli Occupation in 1967, after the Six-Day War between Israel and the Arab states of Jordan, Lebanon, Syria, Iraq, and Egypt (see map 2.1).

[10]Domingo, "Judicial Independence," 152.
[11]Ibid.
[12]Ibid., 156: "[i]n Argentina, only 13 percent of the public have anything good to say about the judiciary; in Peru, 92 percent distrust the judges; in Brazil 70 percent distrust the justice system." In the West Bank over 50% believe the judiciary is doing a bad job.

Map 2.1. Israeli-Occupied Palestinian Territories (1967)

Palestinians living under Israeli Occupation have consistently resisted the presence of Israel in the West Bank and Gaza; the Palestine Liberation Organization—the Palestinian government in exile, headed by Yasir Arafat—gave aid and support to those living in the occupied territories. The 1987 Palestinian Uprising, or Intifada, resulted from the myriad pressures of and Palestinian resistances to occupation.[13] The Intifada helped the Palestinians gain more international support (even from the United States and Israel) for their cause, and it also brought some degree of political legitimacy to both Yasir Arafat, as the leader of the Palestinian people, and his Palestine Liberation Organization.[14] In September of 1993, Yasir Arafat and Israeli prime minister Yitzhak Rabin signed the Oslo Declaration of Principles on the lawn in front of the White House.

The period following Oslo is known as the Interim period; during this time, Palestinian and Israeli leaders were obliged to negotiate a series of solutions to all outstanding, divisive issues.[15] During this period, the PNA, headed by Arafat, obtained full control over 17.2% of the West Bank; this Palestinian-controlled area was designated Area A. Area B, consisting of roughly 23.8% of the West Bank, was under joint Israeli-Palestinian rule. In Area B, Palestinians were responsible for all civilian affairs, while Israel was responsible for security matters. Area C, the remaining 59% of the West Bank, remained under full Israeli control and jurisdiction (see map 2.2).

Compared with the rest of the developing world, the West Bank had a large and diverse set of civic associations; it certainly possessed one of the richest associational landscapes in the Arab world. In 1999, 20% of its population was involved in associational life. Since the signing of the Oslo Accords, international and domestic attention has focused on the development of effective, democratic institutions in the West Bank and Gaza. Adopting the civil society propositions outlined and critiqued in chapter 1, many scholars and policy makers have advocated the development of civic associations. The United Nations Development Programme (UNDP) estimates that in 1992 $174 million in total aid was given to civic sectors in the West Bank; this figure jumped to $263 million in 1993. From 1987 to 1992, the number of Palestinian associations increased from 272 to 444. In 1996, that number was about 1,500.[16]

[13] Civic organizations before, during, and after the Intifada served as key sites of Palestinian mobilization strategies and efforts.

[14] Brand, "The Intifadah and the Arab World."

[15] Such issues include East Jerusalem, Israeli troop redeployments from the West Bank, water allocation, the right of return for Palestinian refugees of 1948 and 1967 and/or refugee repatriation, Israeli settlements on the West Bank, economic cooperation agreements, and borders.

[16] Sullivan, "NGOs in Palestine," 94.

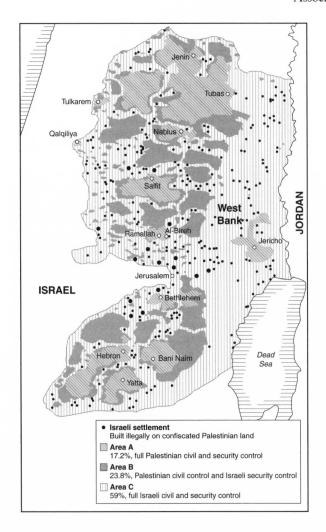

Map 2.2. Palestin-ian-Controlled Areas under Oslo (1995)

Palestinian associational life, however, was not born of either the In-tifada or the Oslo Accords. In fact, the West Bank has a long history of as-sociational life; the earliest Palestinian civic associations can be traced back to the British Mandate. Most of these early associations included re-ligious groups, clubs, labor unions, women's societies, and charitable groups. Some of these associations were family based, such as the Dajani Sports Club in Jerusalem. Others, such as the National Muslim societies and the Orthodox Club, were religion based. A significant number of as-sociational programs focused on social issues transcending immediate fa-milial cleavages. The women's societies were active in addressing illiteracy and carried on workshops on health care.[17] As Lesch points out, "the Jerusalem society opened a welfare center in the Old City in 1931, distributed food to poor families, and sent nurses to help mothers learn proper sanitation methods and care for their children."[18]

Because Palestinians became increasingly resistant to British colonialism, several of these associations became politicized. The Arab Executive Committee, a body of the Palestinian political elite, began mobilizing these associations as part of the larger national struggle against British dominance. Hajj Amin al-Husseini, a member of the Arab Executive Committee, garnered much support from the associational terrain in the 1930s.[19] During the 1936 revolt against the British, these associations played key welfare roles, distributing basic necessities and food items to local populations. As Jewish immigration to Palestine increased and resentment toward the British was compounded, these associations began to play a more direct political role. According to Muslih, "Although the associations tried to serve their particular interests, they also worked for the national cause, and, in many instances, work for the national cause was paramount."[20] This was also true of the emerging Palestinian labor unions of the 1940s, which attempted to ensure that, given the increase in Jewish labor in Palestine, Palestinian labor was protected.[21] The associational infrastructure was disrupted with the creation of the state of Israel in 1948. Many of the Palestinian associations in Haifa, Jaffa, and Jerusalem were simply uprooted. The new associations that would emerge after 1948 were either legacies of past associations—still charitable in outlook—or new associations mobilizing on national concerns. Some of these new associations would reemerge in the West Bank and in Gaza. Several others, however, were resurrected in other parts of the Arab world. Palestinian refugees took with them their civic skills and planted them abroad.[22] According to Brand, "The institutions they revived or reconstructed—womens', teachers', students' and workers' organizations as well as charitable societies—were the natural heirs of pre-1948 institutions."[23]

After the 1948 war with Israel, the West Bank was annexed by Jordan, and Gaza fell under the military administration of Egypt. In the aftermath of the war, over 700,000 Palestinians became refugees; they fled to the West Bank, Gaza, and the Arab countries of Jordan, Lebanon, and Syria. A number of community-based charitable organizations emerged

[17]Muslih, *Origins of Palestinian Nationalism;* Lesch, *Arab Politics in Palestine.*
[18]Lesch, *Arab Politics in Palestine,* 62.
[19]Muslih, *Origins of Palestinian Nationalism,* 260.
[20]Ibid.
[21]Khalaf, *Politics in Palestine,* 38.
[22]Muslih, *Origins of Palestinian Nationalism,* 260.
[23]Brand, *Palestinians in the Arab World,* 3.

in the West Bank to help with the immediate needs of local Palestinian constituents and refugees.[24] Most of these charitable organizations obtained direct funds from other Arab countries, especially those in the Gulf area. The number of community-based associations continued to grow, particularly after Israel occupied the West Bank and Gaza in 1967.

Israeli Occupation led to harsh economic and political circumstances for Palestinians living in the West Bank and Gaza. Politically, Palestinians did not have a right to represent themselves. Israel created Israel-manned military administrative institutions in the West Bank and Gaza to address Palestinian political needs, institutions that would be boycotted during the 1987 Palestinian Uprising. Further, Palestinians were denied basic political freedoms; they could not explicitly deal with anything political. They could not express political opinions, meet for political purposes, or mobilize citizens for political agendas. Political parties and factions were outlawed. Any initiative to organize politically was deemed illegal by Israel; often, those attempting to organize were imprisoned and severely punished.

## PALESTINIAN POLITICAL AND CIVIL LIFE UNDER OCCUPATION

Under Israeli Occupation, the economic situation in the Territories grew bleaker each day. Joost Hiltermann, writing of labor and women's movements during the Intifada, notes that the Palestinian population of the West Bank and Gaza "has not only lived under harsh military occupation; it has also suffered economic exploitation, blocked development, and discrimination in services."[25] With closed borders, and no means of exporting and importing, Israel flooded the markets of the Occupied Territories with Israeli-made goods. And while Israel extracted the Territories' raw materials and exploited its labor force, economic depression and blocked industrialization ensued.

High-growth Israeli sectors, such as food processing, textiles, tourism, and construction, were confronted by a shortage of unskilled labor. With a rapid escalation in population, a shortage of jobs, an underdeveloped industrial sector, and downward-spiraling standards of living, many Palestinians turned to the Israeli economy for employment. In 1968, 5,000 Palestinians from the Occupied Territories worked in Israel; in 1974, there were 69,000, and by 1986, there were 94,700. Other estimates put the Palestinian labor force in Israel as high as 120,000.[26] Israeli business

[24]Brown, *Palestinian Politics after the Oslo Accords.*
[25]Hiltermann, *Behind the Intifada,* 17.
[26]Ibid.

and farm owners employed Palestinian laborers at a fraction of what Israeli workers were paid. According to Emanuel Farjoun, "[t]he average wage of an Israeli worker . . . adds up, together with fringe benefits, to earnings which are twice or three times those of an Arab worker from the Occupied Territories."[27] On the one hand, the economic impact on Palestinian development meant that an increasing number of Palestinians became proletarian; on the other, it meant that Palestinians, when possible, opted to leave the West Bank and Gaza altogether. Forty percent of Palestinian families reported that one or more of their family members lived abroad. This "brain drain" of skilled and university-trained workers further damaged prospects of Palestinian economic development.

Palestinians under Israeli Occupation knew that the occupation was not temporary and that Israel had long-term goals and plans for the future of the West Bank and Gaza. Says Rita Giacaman, a Palestinian academic living in Ramallah, "We knew that the Israeli military was out to possess the land without us people. . . . What we did not know was how to mobilize under occupation, when it was becoming practically impossible to move and do anything at the political or other levels without being subjected to arrests or attacks from the Israeli military."[28] Within this context, a number of community-based associations and societies began to emerge; these associations addressed the immediate economic, social, and political problems facing a new generation of Palestinians living under occupation.

This new generation of Palestinians had essentially grown up facing no other political reality than that offered by Israeli Occupation. Coupled with the consequences of military occupation, many social conditions began to change in the Occupied Territories as well. Education rates were on the rise; however, there were very few domestic prospects of professional careers. The growing number of Palestinian workers in Israel not only experienced firsthand exploitation but also saw the virtues of democratic governance and wanted to be treated like their Israeli counterparts. Further, a newly politicized stratum of elites replaced traditional elites, often seen as tacit accomplices to the Israeli Occupation.[29]

Israel, while not willing to concede the Occupied Territories to the Palestinians or grant them sovereignty, sought to relegate some administrative tasks to the Palestinians. The "Administrative Autonomy" plan of the 1970s, designed by Moshe Dayan, tried to address the Palestinian sit-

---

[27]Farjoun, "Palestinian Workers in Israel," quoted in Hiltermann, *Behind the Intifada*, 23.

[28]Rita Giacaman, quoted in Hiltermann, *Behind the Intifada*, 41.

[29]Robinson, *Building a Palestinian State*, 14. "[Palestinian] notables continued to enjoy a relatively privileged position and were allowed benefits—such as fewer travel restrictions and more easily obtained permits for a variety of activities not extended to most Palestinians."

uation. Under this plan, Israel would retain full control of the Territories, but Palestinians themselves would administrate daily life. A common rhetorical slogan captured Palestinian sentiment toward this Israeli vision: "They [Israel] won't give us liberty, but want us to take care of our own trash." For this plan to work, Israel depended on forging strong ties with Palestinian elites to monitor Palestinian administrative functions.[30]

In the 1970s and 1980s, several factors threatened these traditional Palestinian elite with social marginalization. First, Israeli land confiscations displaced the Palestinian peasantry, over which notable landowners had control. Second, in opening its borders to Palestinian wage laborers, Israel exposed Palestinians to an entirely different political system, where Jewish citizens of Israel enjoyed full democratic rights. And third, the expansion of the middle class through the establishment of a Palestinian university system in 1972 undermined the social and political power of the traditional elite.[31] Palestinian universities became key sites for political mobilization; according to Glenn Robinson in *Building a Palestinian State: The Incomplete Revolution,* "[s]tudent enrollment in the newly opened Palestinian universities expanded sharply in the 1970s and 1980s."[32] In 1977, student enrollment figures were recorded at 2,601; ten years later, nearly 16,000 students were enrolled at major universities.[33] Further, Israeli authorities arrested many political activists, some of whom were nurtured in the heart of these very universities. Israel hoped to keep these activists off the Palestinian streets and unable to initiate any form of political mobilization. This was a grave miscalculation on Israel's part, however; the prison experience in fact galvanized the emergence of new strata of political elites. Most political prisoners taken by Israel during the Intifada, Robinson goes on to note, were "held . . . in the same compound, Ketziot/Ansar III in the Negev desert." He writes, "[t]he list of those imprisoned in the Negev read like a Who's Who of Palestinian political life: student activists, labor leaders, university professors, doctors, journalists, and the like."[34]

Most of the mobilization patterns in the West Bank and Gaza were a direct result of the marginalization of the traditional elites by a political elite newly forged in the crucible of Israeli Occupation. In the absence of

[30]For instance, the Israeli organization of Palestinian municipal elections in the early 1970s was designed to limit the emergence of Palestinian nationalist elite figures. Most of those who assumed municipality positions were among the pro-Jordanian and pro-Israeli Palestinian elites.

[31]Robinson, "The Role of the Professional Middle Class," 321; and Brynen, *A Very Political Economy,* 142, 144.

[32]Robinson, *Building a Palestinian State,* 22.

[33]Ibid.

[34]Ibid.

a governing Palestinian state, new political factions in the Occupied Territories saw themselves as extensions of the PLO in exile. These new movements, led by new social and political elites, prioritized political mobilization as a means of resisting Israeli Occupation. Women's associations, labor unions, student and professional organizations—these and other civic bodies mobilized the previously invisible Palestinian citizenry to political ends. Particularly in the 1980s, as Jamil Hilal notes, "these grass root organizations sought members—as their mother political organizations—from social sectors and classes that were excluded previously from active participation in politics (women, youth, students, workers, and peasants)."[35] Palestinian civic life, in other words, gave Palestinians the voice and the vision to end Israeli Occupation.

Having a political mandate, however, was not sufficient in and of itself to mobilize members toward larger political activities. In fact, many of these movements realized that they had to address key social issues in order to be able to establish larger membership bases and remain competitive among other factions. Liza Taraki, writing of mass organization in the West Bank, argues that occupational pressures forced "the national movement" to either "confine itself to clandestine work," and thereby sacrifice the strength of numbers, or "evolve alternative, open structures that would be more difficult to destroy."[36] Ultimately, the "[national] movement realized that efforts had to be directed to addressing the concrete needs of different sectors of society within the framework of mass organizations."[37] For the Palestinians, then, "taking care of their own trash" allowed them to lay the foundation to massive civic mobilization against the Occupation.

Nationalist movements strategically mobilized the occupied citizenry by addressing the pressing social concerns that were everywhere visible. Women's movements, for instance, found themselves adopting platforms of gender consciousness, addressing the necessity of more equitable treatment of women, and providing seminars and workshops that aimed at raising gender awareness—while also empowering women politically and obtaining support for their factions. Similarly, the students' movements, labor movements, and other unions that were administrated by Palestinian political factions all implemented similar programs. This new movement of political elites included leaders from all factions, Fatah (Arafat's main party), the Democratic Front for the Liberation of Palestine (DFLP), the Popular Front for the Liberation of Palestine (PFLP), and the Communist Party. Palestinian political factions disguised them-

---

[35]Hilal, "State-Society Dynamics under the PNA."
[36]Taraki, "Mass Organizations in the West Bank," 442–43.
[37]Ibid.

selves as social organizations. By the late 1980s, it was common to find four organizations based on factional ties in any given locale. For example, in a single neighborhood district, one would often find four of the same women's associations, four of the same sports clubs, and four of the same student associations, each based on a different political relationship. Because overt political engagement was punishable by imprisonment and even physical violence, political engagement was coded as social engagement. Activists clandestinely represented the citizenry through labor unions, trade associations, women's or student groups, and similar social organizations.[38] One Fatah leader recounts this process of political mobilization through social organization; her description of the social programs implemented to bring women into "the national struggle" is worth citing at length:

> The factions agreed that women needed to be brought into the national struggle. Some women wanted to contribute socially, and we gave them the choice to get involved politically. We introduced ourselves as associations that aim to help our society. Through this mechanism, we screened the qualifications and competencies of young women for political involvement. When we felt these women were qualified, we then approached them to join the faction. How else could we get women involved? . . . We [also] needed to increase women's awareness. So we had to offer them something and provide them with their needs and priorities. Like in the villages, they wanted preschools, and stitching and knitting workshops. We also trained people in first aid and other health awareness programs. We distributed a lot of first-aid kits in the villages and we did this in all neighborhoods because there was no PNA. We started literacy programs for women, taught them about their legal rights, and in the end we used our preschools as sites to politically organize and mobilize women. Once the Intifada started, we began offering help to political prisoners and participated in demonstrations. Then we trained young women to directly help organize political meetings, distribute leaflets, and help with the Intifada. As far as the Israeli Occupation forces were concerned, we were simply a women's association that helped our community.[39]

Thus, Palestinian civil society in the 1980s was based on the goals and aspirations of Palestinian political society. "In effect, the modern organization (professional, relief committees, student blocs, women's com-

[38]Giacaman, "In the Throes of Oslo"; Hiltermann, *Behind the Intifada,* 17; and Abu 'Amr, *Al-Mujtama.*

[39]Amaney Jamal, interview with Fatah activist, West Bank, summer 1999.

mittees, labor unions, and others) that the new elite built in the 1980s,"
as Glenn Robinson writes, "were the 'army' with which the new elite 'took
power.'"[40]

The political movements became very popular for their programs.
While Fatah, at times, was seen as (and criticized for) promoting traditional and clan ties, the leftist groups—the DFLP, PFLP, and the Communist Party—gained widespread support from other national leftist
parties and countries with close ties to the Soviet Union.[41] In spite of factionalism, civil social activity had a clear focus and agenda because the
majority of the Palestinian population focused its efforts on independence and resistance to Israeli Occupation. The PLO in exile largely
funded social programs implemented by factional associations.[42] Although factionalism had become institutionalized, and though there were
many similar organizations with different political ties in each given district, a larger political goal, ending Israeli Occupation, united Palestinian
civil and political society. This unity among the Palestinian political factions, however, would crumble in the post-Oslo phase, only to be replaced
by a polarized associational terrain along the dimensions of support for
or opposition to the PNA.

## ASSOCIATIONAL LIFE POST-OSLO

For many observers, both external and internal, the peace process was
expected to bring the Palestinian people their long-held hopes of statehood and an end to the Israeli Occupation, which had for decades inhib-
ited the Palestinians from achieving their economic, political, and social
potential. For Palestinians, the struggle to end Israeli Occupation was a
national priority. Although a true and just peace has yet to be achieved,
important changes on the ground and their impact on a once vibrant and
lively Palestinian civil society need to be pointed out. In the post-Oslo
phase, the PLO as a quasi-governmental apparatus was now the PNA, a
governmental body within the West Bank and Gaza. Fatah supporters
dominated the vast majority of positions in the ranks of the PNA. The
unification among the different political factions the PLO had enjoyed
as it sought to end Israeli Occupation was no longer guaranteed. In
fact, most of the political Left vehemently disagreed with the Oslo Ac-

---

[40] Robinson, "The Role of the Professional Middle Class," 321.

[41] Fatah maintained close ties to two of the most conservative Arab states, Jordan and
Saudi Arabia, and among Fatah's leaders were members of prominent notable Palestinian
families such as the Husseinis.

[42] Hammami, "NGOs."

cords and felt that Arafat had conceded too much to Israel. The legitimacy the PLO had enjoyed in exile now had to be secured domestically, under the new Palestinian National Authority. The PLO leadership, which for decades had aided and encouraged civic mobilization in Palestine, needed to assert its authority and ensure that the same efforts toward civil society it had encouraged would not turn against itself.

Palestinians paid a heavy price to bring the PLO back from exile. The symbolic significance of Yasir Arafat's return to the Occupied Territories was no small accomplishment; in fact, it was seen as a tremendous victory. Palestinians worldwide viewed Arafat's entrance into Gaza as a triumphant victory for Palestinian perseverance and steadfastness. Were it not for the Intifada's mass revolt and the grassroots strategies of mobilization it had implemented, the Palestinians would not have accredited its leadership with such a grandiose accomplishment.

Once Arafat stepped into Gaza, he had overwhelming tasks ahead of him. On the one hand, he needed to build the groundwork for a Palestinian democratic state. The essence of Palestinian political struggle and consciousness was grounded in a discourse of basic human and democratic rights and freedoms. On the other hand, Arafat, too, had to deliver on his promises to Israel, as part of the Oslo framework, to guarantee Israeli security.[43] Thus, Arafat faced two challenges: to convince Israel that the Palestinian government could deliver security, and to maintain popular support among Palestinians.[44] To control Palestinian dissenters opposed to the Oslo Accords, and to ensure his own preeminence, Arafat brought home his old leadership styles from abroad. Arafat employed leadership strategies of personalism, patronage, and clientelism to oversee both negotiations with Israel and the building of the Palestinian state over which he presided.

The events leading to the Oslo Accords left the PLO factions at odds. The opposition movements of the Left, mainly the DFLP and the PFLP, which had for years maintained their allegiance to and support of the PLO, now found it ideologically contradictory to support the Oslo Accords. They, along with Hamas—which gained widespread support during the Intifada—opposed the Accords. Their political vision did not include a two-state solution with full recognition of Israel's right to exist on Palestinian land. Further, most of the Left felt that Arafat had abandoned them during the Oslo negotiations. The Palestinian opposition elite found themselves marginalized by the Accords and unable to formulate a strategy of opposition in response to the new and expeditious

[43]Abu 'Amr, *Al-Mujtama*. Regarding discussion of the centralized powers required by the Oslo Accords for their implementation. The essence of the Oslo Accords for Israel is the premise of land for security.

[44]Rubin, *The Transformation of Palestinian Politics*.

political developments of the peace process.[45] Thus, many members of the opposition elite found themselves outside the realm of the mainstream political process. As a result, some found it very lucrative to form their own local nongovernmental organizations (NGOs). Donor support for human rights and democracy initiative organizations increased drastically during the first years of the Oslo Accords, and many of the former Left took advantage of these new opportunities. "For many of them [the former Left], their handful of tenuously affiliated NGOs remain the most cohesive and operational aspect of their former movement," says Rema Hammami.[46] With most of the political Left marginalized by Oslo, Fatah and its supporters enjoyed significant latitude in everyday Palestinian politics.

As the PNA began laying the framework for its governing institutions, Arafat began filling bureaucratic posts and positions from a widespread constituent base that had aided the PLO. Now that he was firmly in place as a leader, he felt less obligated to cater to the Palestinian Left. The elimination of the Left from bureaucratic consideration did not make Arafat's job much easier. The ranks of Fatah encompassed multiple constituencies, dedicated loyalists, and eager supporters. Arafat had now to appease his supporters in exile: those who still remembered the horrific Black September in Jordan,[47] the devastating losses of Sabra and Shatila,[48]

---

[45] The leftist factions, as a result, were unprepared to deal with the new Oslo realities. No longer were they opposition movements demanding greater concessions from Israel; rather, they had to reformulate a new strategy with regard to the PNA. While some in the opposition felt it was their national responsibility to support the PNA's efforts, others in the opposition felt that Arafat had given up on the "Palestinian Cause" to legitimize his rule. In the case of the DFLP, a group of supporters of the PNA and Oslo splintered off to form the FIDA movement (Palestine Democratic Union).

[46] Hammami, "NGOs," 54.

[47] Black September is the name given the Jordanian army's September 1970 assault on Palestinian refugees in the refugee camps of Jordan, when it was assumed by the Jordanian monarchy that the PLO was planning a coup d'état against the monarchy. As a result, the PLO left Jordan for Lebanon.

[48] Sabra and Shatila are the Palestinian refugee camps in Lebanon attacked by the Lebanese Phalange militias during the 1982 Israel war in Lebanon. Hundreds of Palestinians, mostly women and children, were chased down and murdered in the streets of these camps. Sabra and Shatila symbolize a humiliating PLO defeat in Lebanon, where the PLO was supposed to protect Palestinian civilians in the camps. Because of international pressure, the PLO negotiated an agreement under the auspices of international observers. The PLO would leave Lebanon so long as the Palestinian refugees were protected from Israeli forces and the Lebanese militias. Close to the time after Arafat and the PLO were escorted out of Lebanon by international peace envoys, the horrific massacres in Sabra and Shatila took place. Being trumpeted out of Lebanon was humiliating enough for the PLO, but for the United States to fail to deliver on its promises to protect Palestinian civilians was a tremendous and devastating blow to the PLO. The PLO did not recover from its experience in Lebanon until the Palestinian Intifada gave it new breath.

and the days of political stagnation in Tunisia.[49] He also needed to satisfy his internal partners and defenders in the West Bank and Gaza, who gave the PLO life after its Tunisian exile. Internally, Arafat supporters came from a wide spectrum. The Palestinian intelligentsia, including Hanan A'shrawi, Faysal al-Husayni, Haydar Abd al-Shaf'i Ghassan al-Khatib, and Saib 'Urayqat served as his appointed delegation to the joint Jordanian-Palestinian delegation at the Madrid Peace Talks, which were sponsored by the G.W.H. Bush administration. They also instituted a public relations campaign in the Western media for their leader and the Cause. The thousands of Fatah youth supporters who were serving sentences in Israeli jails for their Intifada-related activities also awaited recognition for their efforts. Hundreds of Fatah loyalists had also been deported for their activities against Israeli Occupation. They, too, eagerly waited to return, hoping to take part in the new Palestinian leadership. Additionally, notable and wealthy families that had maintained close ties, both financially and ideologically, to Fatah expected acknowledgment from Arafat for their years of dedication. The task was tedious. But in order to maintain his personalistic style of leadership, Arafat created an expanded bureaucracy, multiple security agencies, and an overstaffed police force.

Arafat moved swiftly, appointing supporters to cabinet and ministerial positions. Former Intifada Fatah youth supporters rapidly occupied the ranks of security and police forces.[50] After his decisive electoral victory in 1996, Arafat continued to expand positions and posts in his cabinet and ministries to appoint followers. The number of ministries grew from fourteen in 1994 to twenty-three in 1996.

Stylistically, Arafat did not deal well with criticism; he did not hesitate to reprimand his critics. As Amal Jamal notes, he "silenced critics, co-opted enemies and ostracized dissenters by either integrating them into the government or marginalizing them."[51] He kept power fully centralized under his direct executive control, granting himself legislative decrees

---

[49]After the PLO left Lebanon, it set up its base in Tunisia. But there it appeared that the PLO had stagnated, with no clear political vision or rejuvenation. The Soviet Union, a PLO supporter, was losing its battle in the Cold War, and Arab domestic leaders realigned themselves with the United States. The United States was not a PLO supporter, and it therefore appeared that Arafat would remain in Tunisia endlessly. In fact, the defeat in Lebanon, and the PLO's stagnation in Tunisia, led many Palestinians in the Occupied Territories to believe that they had to take matters into their own hands if they were ever to end Israeli Occupation.

[50]Shain and Sussman, "From Opposition to State-Building," 289. As Shain and Sussman argue, "[t]he large security force and bureaucracy create a neo-patrimonial social contract by putting many people on the public pay roll and precluding potential opposition."

[51]Amal Jamal, "State-Building, Institutionalization and Democracy," 13; and Rex Brynen, "The Neo-patrimonial Dimension to Palestinian Politics."

that would allow him to bypass the legislative process.[52] Although the Palestinian Legislative Council had been popularly elected in 1996, it had very little authority or autonomy. It spent hours on end legislating and passing resolutions, but Arafat ratified only a few. To the dismay of many, the Palestinian leader monitored every facet of Palestinian political life. As Abu Ziyadah of the PNA's Planning Ministry noted, "Arafat busies himself with small details which he should not be handling. He should not be issuing building permits for another house or floor. He should not be holding meetings with all and sundry. He is having a bad influence on the behavior of his ministries. He constantly interferes with their work and the work of the senior bureaucracy."[53]

Arafat's tasks of nation building were almost impossible. That negotiations with Israel were very slow and showing little progress made matters much more difficult. After a series of Hamas-sponsored suicide attacks in Israel in 1995–96, Prime Minister Yitzhak Rabin's assassination in 1995, and the election of Israeli right-winger Benjamin Netanyahu in 1996, the peace process staggered along. Throughout these wearying negotiations, the PNA was also trying to create a state, one that the continuing Israeli Occupation made quite difficult. Arafat's long list of state-building tasks demonstrated just how much there was to be done. This list, according to Barry Rubin, included building "a legal system, infrastructure, job programs, economic production, agriculture, a social security and educational system; finding export markets; attracting capital from abroad for investment; rehabilitating freed prisoners; developing health and childhood and women's projects; and organizing village councils and city government."[54] Further, the PNA "also needed to complete the establishment of the main institutions such as the judiciary, the monetary authority, the development bank, the housing bank, the water authority, the energy authority, and the land authority."[55] The list, it seemed, was endless.

Palestinians gradually became aligned with one of two camps: those who were sympathetic with the enormous tasks in front of Arafat's PNA, and those who resented his undemocratic methods and personalistic style. Supporters of the PNA argued that the Palestinian people should be patient with and supportive of the PNA during this critical period in Palestinian history. They maintained that democratic critics were aiming to destabilize the PNA and bring it shame in the face of arduous nego-

---

[52]Amal Jamal, "State-Building, Institutionalization and Democracy"; Brown, *Palestinian Politics after the Oslo Accords.*

[53]Abu-Amr Ziad, quoted in Rubin, *The Transformation of Palestinian Politics,* 3.

[54]Rubin, *The Transformation of Palestinian Politics,* 11.

[55]Ibid.

tiations with Israel. Unity, they argued, should be a national priority.[56] Critics of the PNA, however, disagreed. They wanted to lay the foundations of democracy as expeditiously as possible. They feared that Arafat's leadership style was inherently undemocratic, and most of his democratic concessions were in fact cosmetic overtures to appease citizens. If and when a Palestinian state emerged, the basic structure of a democratic system of governance, they argued, should already be in place. Many critics believed that without full democratic governance, a state could never come into existence in the first place. High-profile Palestinian intellectuals such as Ghassan al-Khatib articulated these sentiments. The PNA's "poor performance," he said, "leaves the Palestinian position vulnerable." This is "particularly the case," he continued, "when the criticism concerns issues on which Israel was formerly criticized, i.e., human rights, development, etc., because it then eases some of the continuing pressure in Israel for its practices against the Palestinians."[57] PNA opponents did not take their criticisms too far, however. Public support for Arafat was high, although it would later steadily decline, and the opposition feared political repercussions and public denunciation.

## CORRUPTION, PATRONAGE, CLIENTELISM, AND THE PNA

Because Arafat's tactics of rewarding followers and sanctioning defectors in the West Bank had expanded during the Oslo Accords, clientelistic networks grew. It was far easier, for example, to obtain the necessary paperwork to build a house by seeking the help of a clientelistic tie (or *wasta*) than it was to go directly to the government. Further, Yasir Arafat not only extended rewards to his followers but in many cases also employed them, thereby extending patrimonial privileges to his supporters. In 1999, the World Bank estimated that Yasir Arafat employed over 100,000 Palestinians in the Palestinian National Authority, or close to 25% of the total Palestinian workforce.[58] As Shain and Sussman argue, "[t]he large security force and bureaucracy create a neo-patrimonial social contract by putting many people on the public pay roll." They go on to contend that this form of patronage "preclud[es] potential opposition."[59] Arafat's monopoly on the resources and unchecked power to reward and punish Palestinians allowed him to exert his influence over every Palestinian. His supporters received jobs, permits, and contracts for

[56]Ibid., 3.
[57]Ghassan al-Khatib, quoted in Rubin, *The Transformation of Palestinian Politics,* 53.
[58]World Bank, *West Bank and Gaza in Brief.*
[59]Shain and Sussman, "From Opposition to State-Building."

themselves and their families, while his opponents faced harassment and sanctions against their economic interests and families.[60] The costs of opposing Arafat were certainly higher than the costs of supporting him.[61] In this environment, associations that were sympathetic to the PNA were afforded rights and privileges that non-PNA-supporting associations were not able to obtain.[62]

It is not surprising, therefore, that political corruption and clientelism grew out of Arafat's attempts to solidify and centralize a strong political base through patronage and clientelistic networks. In an article on economic repercussions post-Oslo, Sara Roy writes that "[a]llegiance to Arafat rather than technocratic skills quickly became the primary avenue to power and status."[63] Allegations of corruption among public officials increased and were seldom accounted for. Several sources began to indicate that senior members of the PNA were exporting money into anonymous accounts in Geneva and New York.[64] Similarly, domestic frustration with political corruption was on the rise. Based on polls of the Center of Palestine Research Studies in Nablus, 68.2% in 1999 felt that there was widespread corruption in the ranks of the PNA; three years earlier, 49.3% of Palestinians polled felt the same way. By 2004, this percentage had risen to 85%. Only 7% felt that they did not need a *wasta* to find employment. The Palestinian security and police forces continued to abuse their power and operate above society, rather than serving the local community. Arafat often catered to his security personnel, and he came down hard on critics of his power base.

By and large, political corruption had remained unchecked in the newly administered Palestinian territories during the Oslo time period. The international community had more or less turned a blind eye to PNA corruption. Political corruption had spiraled in multiple directions, retarding democratic development in the process. Primarily, it polarized Palestinian society; there were those who had access to the clientelistic and patron networks of the PNA, and there were those who did not. This selective representation had undermined the legitimacy of the PNA as a governing institution; hence, support for the regime declined gradually since the signing of Oslo. To finance its political networks, the PNA not only played a direct role in the monopolization of industrial sectors but also mishandled donor money. In one such instance, Arafat diverted European donor money designated for building apartments for the poor in

[60] Roy, "Gaza."
[61] Rubin, *The Transformation of Palestinian Politics,* 25.
[62] Roy, "Gaza," 24.
[63] Roy, "Palestinian Society and Economy," 7.
[64] Bergman, "How Much PA Corruption Is too Much?"

Gaza, instead using it to construct luxury apartments for his officials. Similarly, Arafat and his lieutenants had special budget accounts for profits earned by cigarette, cement, gravel, flour, and steel monopolies. Few of Arafat's accounting methods were legitimate, and no paperwork documenting these methods was to be found in any given office or building.[65] In May of 1997, the PNA's own Public Monitoring Department (PMD) claimed in a detailed report that the PNA had used approximately $329 million in irregular expenditures by PNA institutions and official bribes. "In short," says Rex Brynen, "much P[N]A decision making has been driven not by concerns about economic efficiency but by consideration of political consolidation."[66] By strengthening the PNA through patronage and corruption, the PNA's executive branch had a significant power edge over the Palestinian Legislative Council, and Arafat remained unconstrained by the judiciary.

## THE PNA AND THE PLC

The September 1993 Oslo peace agreement called for, among other things, an elected Palestinian representative body to draft a Palestinian constitution. Accordingly, in 1996, the Palestinian Legislative Council (PLC), with its eighty-eight newly elected council members, was delegated the role of drafting the Basic Law. When the Legislative Council began discussion, however, council members "soon found themselves," as Nathan Brown has commented, "engaged in a very public confrontation with Yasir Arafat."[67] Arafat claimed that the council had no right to discuss the Basic Law that would govern Palestinians everywhere. If the Basic Law were to apply to Palestinians everywhere, Arafat preferred that the pre-Oslo PLO structures draft the Basic Law. According to Arafat, the PLC was in charge only of West Bank and Gaza Palestinians, not Palestinians everywhere—that was the PLO's responsibility. Therefore, Arafat wanted PLO structures where *he*—and not the PLC—had solid support to discuss the provisions of a Palestinian Basic Law. Brown goes on to comment on this apparent double standard: "[m]any suspected that Arafat's autocratic tendencies motivated his procedural concerns. Council members with a strong interest in human rights and democracy had no wish to have the contents of the law dictated by Arafat."[68] The PLC in fact became a forum where the exchange of exciting and meaningful

[65]Brynen, *A Very Political Economy,* 142, 144.
[66]Ibid.
[67]Brown, "Constituting Palestine."
[68]Ibid.

debate took place, but little of these public deliberations had a direct, tangible impact on Palestinian citizens. Indeed, the PNA would even block the airing of the Palestinian legislative negotiations when it felt that the subjects debated were sensitive. The PLC, practically rendered impotent by Arafat's overwhelming executive arm, gradually emerged as another democratic decorative ornament. A Center for Palestine Research Studies report had this to say: "By being forced to back down repeatedly—largely because the majority of members basically did support the government—the PLC lost credibility with Arafat and the public's respect."[69] So ludicrous was the PLC's powerlessness that Haydar Abd al-Shafi, a popularly elected parliament member and intellectual elite member of the Intifada, called the PLC a "joke" and resigned.

Elected in 1996, the Palestinian legislature believed that it would play as key and dignified a role in the formation of a Palestinian constitution as did the Founding Fathers of the United States. The underpinning of democracy that they envisioned would be a legislative branch that could hold the PNA executive accountable. So ambitious was their image of democratic governance that the PLC attempted to implement a governmental structure that far exceeded the legislative autonomy in any given Arab state. Says Rubin, the PLC's proposals "tipped the balance toward the legislature even more than did the American system."[70] The Palestinian legislature was left utterly disappointed. Arafat announced himself the eighty-ninth member of the eighty-eight-member elected Palestinian parliament. Often, Arafat even sat in the Speaker's chair, to assert his leadership in the branch. Draft law after draft law—indeed hundreds of laws—were sent to President Arafat and never ratified. Arafat immediately viewed the PLC as a fierce competitor and treated it as such. Relationships became even more strained when the PLC demanded an investigation into allegations of PNA corruption. Businesses began complaining that they could not effectively compete in the market, because of Arafat's evident favoritism toward monopolies such as the Palestinian National Company for Economic Development, the Petrol Board, and the Tobacco Company. PNA officials used their public positions to grant their own businesses licenses and government subsidies, while security officers used their powers to intervene in economically advantageous ways.[71] Without an effective legislative or judicial body to place constraints on the PNA, its abuses of power continued to grow.

[69]CPRS, evaluations of the Legislative Council's first year, quoted in Rubin, *The Transformation of Palestinian Politics*, 44.

[70]Rubin, *The Transformation of Palestinian Politics*, 29.

[71]Ibid., 42; Adel Samara, "Globalization, the Palestinian Economy and the Society Since Oslo," *Journal of Palestine Studies* 33.3 (2000): 20–34.

## Rule of Law, the Judiciary, and the PNA

Palestinian rule of law remained weak owing to both the history of colonialism in the region and Arafat's resistance to adopting legal provisions that would place limits on his power. A plethora of legal edicts and decrees reflected the long history of Palestine's occupation by outside powers, dating back to the time of the Ottoman Empire, the British Mandate, and Israel. After the war of 1948, Gaza fell under the legal jurisprudence of Egypt, while the West Bank fell under that of Jordan. In the post-1967 period, a mixture of Israeli law and the Islamic Shariah law applied. Under the PNA, any legal code had yet to be firmly adopted. Clear legal provisions and jurisdictions had not been institutionalized. Executive decree—that is, Arafat's ability to veto, legislate, and adjudicate—was strong in the case of the West Bank. Arafat's refusal (until 2002) to sign the Basic Law, which would have outlined the powers of the executive, legislative, and judicial branches, was similar to the reasons many Arab and authoritarian leaders give for not enforcing constitutional provisions that deal with citizen representation: Arafat viewed the Palestinian Constitution as a tool of asserting his rule, but was less willing to adopt a constitution that placed limits on his authority.[72]

The PNA consistently ignored PLC legislation, disregarded High Court rulings, and dismissed judges that did not uphold PNA standards. Further, the PNA established security courts that prosecuted suspects without trials. The executive continued to defy court rulings and undermined the professional independence of judges and lawyers. The High Court and the attorney general were anything but independent, as Yasir Arafat oversaw their jurisdiction. Since the courts had very little autonomy or power to adjudicate, public confidence in these institutions rapidly declined. This lack of trust in the judicial system further strengthened the executive, to whom the public turned for reparations that it would otherwise have secured from the courts.[73]

Instead of establishing a system of independent courts and judiciaries, Arafat created, in 1995, a High State Security Court composed of military judges with no defined jurisdiction or procedure. Soon thereafter came the frightening accounts of "moonlight" courts; defendants appeared in court at night for a few minutes and were sentenced with no representation. Accompanying these accounts were stories of torture and

---

[72]Hammami, "NGOs"; Bisharah, *Musahama fi Naqd al-Mujtam'a al-Madani;* Salim, *Al-Munazamat;* Ibrahim, "Crises, Elites, and Democratization," for discussion on state-society relations and the weak rule of law in the Arab world.

[73]LAW, "Executive Interference in the Palestinian Judiciary."

disappearances.[74] Freedom House Indicators show that civil and political liberties remained extremely low since 1996. In fact, these indicators illustrate that the civic and political liberties in the West Bank were comparable to those of most authoritarian regimes across the developing world, earning the West Bank a ranking of "Not Free."[75]

In November of 1999, twenty well-known Palestinian personalities, nine of whom were Palestinian Legislative Council (PLC) members, issued a statement that became known as the Petition-20. This statement accused Arafat's administration of "opening the door to opportunists who are spreading corruption throughout Palestinian society."[76] In response, the PLC—in which most legislators were Fatah members—condemned these nine members and argued that President Arafat should be immune to all criticism because he was a symbol for the Palestinian people. Further, eight of the signatories were arrested, while two were held under house arrest, though later released. Two PLC members were attacked by unidentified assailants: Mu'awiyah al-Misri was shot in his foot, and 'Abd al-Jawad Salih was beaten in a Jericho demonstration.[77] On 1 December 1999, Palestinian politicians, NGO leaders, and other public figures responded, releasing a well-circulated, public communiqué asking Arafat to exercise his power democratically. Even in the most critical times of Palestinian hardship, such as the Aqsa Intifada, prominent Palestinian spokespersons such as Hanan Ashrawi called for implementation of the rule of law. In a 2001 article for *Media Monitors,* she asserts, "[t]he most fundamental requirement for sustaining the very fabric of life in Pales-

---

[74] "Defying the Rule of Law." As *Amnesty International* reported in 1999: "Hundreds of political detainees are currently held in Palestinian prisons and detention centers without charge or trial. Most of these prisoners have now been held for over a year, some for more than four years, outside the framework of local Palestinian law and in violation of international human rights standards. The Palestinian Authority has undermined the rule of law by defying Palestinian High Court Judgments requiring the release of individual prisoners. It also has ignored calls by the Palestinian Legislative Council (PLC) and local human rights organizations and individual Palestinians appealing for the release of prisoners who have been held without due process. In January 1999, the PLC passed a resolution recommending that the Palestinian Authority cancel political detention. In the same month hundreds of Palestinians protested on the streets of various West Bank towns in support of a hunger strike by political prisoners, held for years, without trial, in Jneid Prison and Jericho military Prison. Around 40 individuals are said to have been released; hundreds remain detained. In all parts of the world the judiciary should act as a vital safeguard of the rights of the individual; in the Palestinian Authority the sidelining of the normal system of justice has dangerously injured individual freedoms."

[75] Based on data gathered between 1996 and 2000, Freedom House assigned the West Bank a score of only 6 (the lowest possible) for civil liberties.

[76] Petition circulated in 1999.

[77] Brown, "Constituting Palestine," 101.

tine is the enactment of the principle of the rule of law, particularly in reforming and revitalizing an independent judicial system and in ensuring due process in all cases."[78]

## ASSOCIATIONAL LIFE AND PNA CORRUPTION

The developing world is plagued with the inefficiencies and authoritarian ills of corrupt regimes. Scholars argue that regime corruption has hindered prospects of democratization across the globe. Yet these same scholars are quick to realize that, in most instances, alternatives to strong—albeit corrupt—regimes forecast state collapse. These scholars argue that consolidation of the state should, in many cases, take precedence over democratic reforms that may leave that state in shambles.[79]

Hence, many states continue to prioritize regime consolidation over democratic separation of powers. Through consolidation, leaders can dictate the dispersal of power and strategically spread responsibility. By keeping political institutions centralized, executives have direct control over the entire political landscape. Clientelistic techniques, whereby supporters are rewarded and defectors punished, are built into this notion of strengthening the state. In the case of the PNA, Arafat repeatedly attempted to legitimize his tactics as necessary to ensure Palestinian survivability. Without a strong state, he warned, predators would chip away at what remained of a Palestinian political community.[80] In addition to his already established patron-client style of political leadership, the ongoing Israeli Occupation of the remaining West Bank and the once promising peace negotiations gave Arafat an almost noncontestable base from which to create and subsidize his regime. Other developments in the Middle East, too, had a similar impact on the ability of the PNA to rapidly consolidate one of the largest bureaucratic regimes per capita in the world. Arafat was deeply frustrated that Syria continued to support Palestinian opposition groups. A strong opposition made it all the more difficult for Arafat to convince or coerce the opposition to join the PNA. These groups perpetuated costly violence against Israel, which led to border

[78]Ashrawi, "Lawlessness and the Rule of Law."

[79]See, for examples, Ottaway, "Democratization in Collapsed States"; and Huntington, *Political Order in Changing Societies.*

[80]Many states, especially those emerging from periods of prolonged war, occupation, or state collapse, use such national appeal to justify the corrupt nature of their rule. Many postcolonial states have resorted to similar behavior and built their clientelistic and patron-based states on the logic of protection from outside predators.

closures between PNA-controlled territories. Further, these Israeli closures cost the PNA billions of dollars, depressing the Palestinian GNP to all-time lows.[81] Increased closures led to a greater Palestinian demand on the PNA for social services and employment. The PNA saw its growing bureaucracy as a means of improving the direct welfare of local citizens. "We have 36,000 people [in the security apparatus] of whom we only need 10,000," said Muhammad Dahlan, head of the PNA Preventive Security in Gaza. "This huge number is burden on the P[N]A and is a burden on the security organ. We view it as a social issue because I cannot tell a political prisoner who has spent 15 years in the jail, that I do not have a job for him." Often, the PNA justified its expansive bureaucracy as a measure to appease the United States and Israel. Since the Oslo Accords dictated that the PNA rein in Hamas, the PNA needed a strong, centralized base of power.

The PNA also rationalized its centralization in terms of the need to be strong in the face of other, external Arab foes. Arab states did not prioritize a Palestinian-Israeli negotiated settlement as part of their normalization proposals with Israel. Egypt's Hosni Mubarak, a leader among Arab states, emphasized the need of a Syrian-Israeli peace treaty and rarely mentioned progress on the Israeli-Palestinian front. The Jordanians also embraced the ongoing peace halfheartedly, while anxiously considering the impact of the final outcome. With over 50% of its population of Palestinian decent, Jordanians feared that its Palestinian citizens would forge strong allegiances to a Palestinian state and further destabilize the already economically depressed monarchy. The PNA privately believed that Jordan did not support a Palestinian state and claimed that Jordan was allowing Hamas too much freedom in its kingdom. Angered by its circumvention of King Hussein's presentation to Israel of a proposed Hamas cease-fire in 1997, the PNA became even more skeptical about Jordanian intentions.[82] Arafat's "kiss of death" to Saddam Hussein after Iraq occupied Kuwait in 1990 left Kuwait and Saudi Arabia less willing to aid the PNA in its state-building efforts. In the PNA's assessment, the Palestinians, left alone to deal with the harsh realities of the Israeli Occupation, should have rallied their support behind Arafat and the PNA government, since the rest of the world—even the Arab world—had turned its back on the cause of Palestinian liberation.

[81]Shaban, "The Harsh Reality of Closure," 51. Cumulative losses reached $775 million between 1993 and 1996. When including losses in income by Palestinians working in Israel, that amount reaches $2.815 billion.

[82]Similar disagreements between the PNA and Jordan, such as which regime should have control over the Muslim holy sites in Jerusalem, created more tension between the two nations.

CONCLUSION

In the years after Oslo, Arafat's power grew drastically in the Territories. Owing to the centralized, authoritarian, clientelistic nature of Arafat's rule, civic associations found themselves having to negotiate an environment that limited many of their activities. In the absence of a protected sphere where political parties could function freely, civic organizations continued to be key sites for political and civic participation. To gain support among citizens, many opposition leaders and PNA supporters turned to associations to spread their political visions. By offering programs such as sports clubs, charities, and empowerment workshops, these organizations attempted to gain support for pro-PNA or anti-PNA political programs. Thus, associations in the West Bank either reinforced direct ties to the PNA and its clientelistic networks, or they further distanced members from the PNA and its multiple levels of bureaucratic rule.

The PNA's rule extended to all facets of Palestinian daily life. Associations that once were either politicized along factional ties or apolitical in scope found themselves in a new environment, one that reshaped their programmatic initiatives and financial opportunities. For many associations, gaining political access to the PNA was a financial necessity—not a luxury. For other associations, aiding the national project meant de facto recognition of the PNA's efforts to lead the Palestinians out of decades of misery. Still other associations in the West Bank operated from a core framework of democratic beliefs. The next chapter charts the contours of associational life in the West Bank and its relationships to the manifold political institutions of the PNA during the Oslo period that ultimately influenced patterns of civic engagement of Palestinian association members.

# CHAPTER THREE

# The Polarization of Palestinian Associational Life

DURING THE OSLO PERIOD, Palestinian civic associations were clearly divided into pro- and anti-PNA groups, a polarization that occurred in the wake of the creation of the PNA in 1993 following the Oslo Accords. The sources underlying this dichotomization are in fact multifaceted, encompassing a plethora of interests, factional allegiances, and political ideologies. The classification of associational life along these two main axes offers a political contextual framework through which to analyze the impact of associational life on civic engagement. It is these interactions that influence the quality and content of civic engagement among association members.

As the governing institution with the power to allocate resources to civic associations, and as an authoritarian state, the PNA afforded clientelistic opportunities to its supporters and limited the availability of those opportunities to nonsupporters. Leaders of pro-PNA associations, who were able to exploit the opportunities offered by the PNA's vertically structured clientelistic networks, *reproduced* vertically structured relationships within their own organizations and delivered political support. This chapter demonstrates that the character of the political regime and, indeed, the levels of polarization shape the associational landscape. In such strong centralized contexts, like the West Bank, states mold societies.

This chapter first traces the ways clientelism structured the Palestinian associational landscape, thus polarizing that terrain into pro- and anti-PNA camps. Second, this chapter discusses three interrelated themes that explain the types of associations that have achieved clientelistic access to the PNA: the bolstering of Fatah as the PNA's political party, attitudes about the Oslo Peace Process with Israel, and perceptions of the role donor aid played in shaping Palestinian national and political discourse. Associations supportive of Fatah and Oslo, and that had financial needs met by the PNA, tended to have access to the PNA through informal patron-client channels. Although the reasons for these associations' support varied along these different dimensions, they were all pro-PNA associations. The levels of civic engagement among their members qualitatively differed from the civic engagement of members in anti-PNA associations. Members in anti-PNA associations who opposed Oslo and supported a political faction other than Fatah were unable to access the clientelistic gateways linked to the PNA.

## THE PALESTINIAN ASSOCIATIONAL TERRAIN

As the PNA consolidated its institutions after 1993, it remained wary of the substantial associational presence in Palestine. Without delay, the PNA began to monitor associational activities, to demand a portion of the funding these associations received, and to play a more visible role in daily associational life. A leading official at the Palestinian Ministry of Planning and Economic Cooperation, commenting on the "overextended" role of Palestinian civic associations, said, "Before Oslo these associations had honorable roles. They used to play the role of government, political parties and development."[1] Then, in a frustrated tone, he alluded to the potential competition between the PNA and the civic sector: "Today, they still want to play all these roles."

From the late 1940s through the 1990s, local community associations mushroomed across the West Bank and Gaza. In 1999 Palestine's 1,500 associations encompassed a multitude of programs and agendas.[2] They included charitable societies and welfare associations; trade, student, and workers' unions; professional associations; popular national committees, including women's and student associations; local cooperatives; and donor-funded democracy NGOs, research institutes, think tanks, and advocacy groups.[3] Women's societies, youth societies, resident cooperatives, and village associations were the dominant associational players in local contemporary Palestinian civic life, while charitable and community-based associations by far outnumbered other professional, donor-supported organizations that aspired to generate democratization. Professional, Western-funded organizations, numbering about 120, were more visible and garnered more exposure in the media and in local affairs, but these high-profile organizations—mostly think tanks or research centers—had little contact with their communities on a regular basis[4] and no membership bases.[5] The contact they did have with community members usually took the form of workshops or seminars in which citizens were taught, for example, "the ABCs of good citizenship"; the organizations announced

[1] Amaney Jamal, interview with NBJ, 1999.
[2] See, for a detailed discussion of the Palestinian associational landscape, Brown, *Palestinian Politics after the Oslo Accords,* 148–90.
[3] Brynen, *A Very Political Economy,* 49; Abu 'Amr, *Al-Mujtama.*
[4] Hammami, "NGOs."
[5] Jad, Johnson, and Giacaman, "Transit Citizens," 77. See also Hammami, "NGOs."

their workshops in ads taken out in Palestinian newspapers. Their missions were multifaceted: raising citizen awareness, reporting and exposing government inefficiencies and abuses of power, and guaranteeing the rights of Palestinians.

Once its specific program was executed, such an organization most likely never saw its workshop participants again, so these workshops did little to consistently bring community members together. Local community-based associations, on the other hand, did create a forum that sustained day-to-day interactions, providing space where citizens could learn from and work with one another. In this regard, local community-based charitable organizations provided platforms for communal civic engagement. Most of the associations in the present analysis center on local community-based civic groups.

Charitable associations in 1999 numbered around 500 in the West Bank and Gaza, and they aimed to address the material, psychological, and social needs of local constituents. These organizations targeted a wide variety of individuals living in the immediate proximity of the association, although the actual programs and initiatives deployed were quite similar across institutional, social, and traditional contexts. For example, much charitable work aimed at creating jobs or alternative skills for members so that they could earn sufficient incomes.

These associations also generated money for charitable redistributive purposes through baking and selling desserts, cheese and spinach pies, and other delicacies. Charitable societies offered homes not only to Palestinian art and culture but also to those constituents who could benefit from institutional assistance. Many charitable societies trained members to embroider traditional wares, offering courses to women on how to stitch silk dresses, souvenirs, and similar decorative items. Some organizations marketed these wares, paying members per bundle (or *tuba*) of silk stitched, while others expected members to volunteer their time. With central heating a rarity, these associations also produced sweaters for the needy. Through their redistributive programs, charitable societies created associational communities by forging common interests and purposes.

When local members faced severe financial crisis, they immediately sought the help of their local charitable association. Some associations were self-sufficient and could offer immediate relief, accumulating and dispersing funds at critical times; when schools opened in September, associational monies helped families buy school-related items such as backpacks and pencils. Others had committee members that solicited donations from prosperous members of society to help those facing hardship. Still other associations had direct links to the PNA and were able to secure funds for their members through those channels. They also generated monies that were then redistributed to those in financial need. During Ramadan, the Muslim holy month, charitable associations distributed funds so families could afford to buy meat, chicken, and rice.

Some Palestinian charitable organizations were also extensions of well-established international groups such as the YMCA and YWCA. These types of social clubs were scattered throughout the West Bank and Gaza. Among the other types of West Bank associations were groups that focused on specific issues, such as ensuring that the water supplies to villages were sufficient, developing agricultural sectors, and providing platforms where members with college degrees could meet and discuss academic issues. Numbering around 200, these associations had relatively narrow agendas. There were approximately 350 sports and social clubs in Palestine.

There remained several hundred associations that were extensions of Palestinian factions. Because the Oslo Accords provided governmental institutions for Fatah and PLO supporters, members of other factions, less supportive of the PNA, clung to their former civic associations both to maintain their political allegiances and to counter the prevailing PNA discourse. Confronted with a PNA-controlled media, members of the opposition saw their associations as the only safe haven from which to address PNA propaganda. Through civic involvement, these associations disseminated information that was critical of Oslo and the PNA. Pro-PNA and pro-Fatah associations, on the other hand, used their organizations to generate support for Arafat's government, for instance, by using their sites for PNA employment opportunities. Regardless of factional ties, these associations created and fostered platforms where workers, university students, and women met to discuss issues of immediate concern to Palestinians. They offered summer camps, awareness workshops, first-aid tutorials, and health awareness activities, as did other charitable groups and societies.

There were immediate benefits to associational participation: new opportunities, new communities, and new goals. Although members did benefit from the services of associations, the substantial majority of associational members participated in associational life to improve their local communities. Those who did obtain skills were also expected to contribute their time to the association. Volunteers often facilitated associational involvement by visiting members of the community, discussing local issues, and reporting on their findings. Associations thereby acquired information about addressing and improving immediate community problems and concerns. Members of associations together designed programs and initiatives to meet the needs of the community. All this stood in the larger service of aiding Palestinian society.

In my research, I spoke to association leaders about their activities, their reasons for participating in voluntary work, and their goals and aspirations for their associations. One common theme motivated the association leaders: to improve Palestinian civil, social, and political life. In some small way, these leaders saw themselves as agents of development and change leading to a better Palestine. As one association leader states, "I am convinced that my efforts will benefit society."[6]

But the leaders and the associations also recognized that to succeed, they needed resources. They recognized that they did not exist in a vacuum; they understood that their visions and objectives would have to take into account the current Palestinian political realities that both shaped their programs and determined the success of their projects. Not one interview I conducted omitted mention of the direct or indirect role of the PNA and its institutions in civic life. Some associations viewed their goals and the PNA's as one: hand in hand, they sought to build a Palestinian state. Others felt that their work was seriously hampered by the PNA and its corruption. Many leaders of these oppositional associations focused their energies on standing up to the government's authoritarian tactics. Each type of association related to, interacted with, and influenced member beliefs about the PNA differently.

Those under the protection of the government were guaranteed some form of political access, financial perquisites, and responsiveness from the PNA. In the post-Oslo period, it became customary to see local ads in the daily newspapers taken out by civic associations thanking Yasir Arafat and his PNA for the generous support he bestowed on these associations. After the PNA exempted members of one Jericho-based agricultural association from paying taxes on their agricultural produce, for instance, the association took out the following ad in the daily newspaper *al-Ayyam:* "The Jericho agricultural society, which was just exempt from paying enormous taxes on its produce, offers its gratitude and best wishes to all those responsible in the PNA and to he, who heads them, Mr. President, Yasir Arafat."[7]

This form of relationship—largely based on patron-client relations made possible by the concentration of political power and weakness in the rule of law—appeared "corrupt" to many, despite their participation in it. Only those who had positive government contact could receive services. Witnessing and experiencing this kind of corruption had become a fact of daily life in the Palestinian territories. One leader put it quite succinctly: "The PNA is in and everybody wants to be on the . . . payroll."[8]

"The PNA is now a part of civil society and tries to get involved in every small and big issue" said one leader of a village association. "It is

[6]Amaney Jamal, interview with anti-PNA association members, DAJ, 1999.
[7]*Alal-Ayyam* (2 February 1997). Quoted in Hilal, *al-Nizam al-Siyasi al-Filastini ba'da Uslu.*
[8]Amaney Jamal, interview with anti-PNA association leader JAD, 1999.

in our trade unions, teacher's unions and civil society organizations."[9] With such a visible role in civic affairs, it was difficult to distinguish between state and social sectors. In some ways, despite its vibrancy and multiplicity, Palestinian civil society had become an extension of the government. As such, much of the tension that occurred between the PNA and its dissenters remained confined to the realm of civil society and never reached the institutions of government. Pro-PNA civic actors defended their government, while anti-PNA associations cast accusations and documented government corruption. As the forces of civil society battled it out, the PNA remained isolated and protected from the voice of its critics—and it remained in control of essential resources.

Absent a viable, enforceable system of checks and balances, controlling the quick spread of corruption in the ranks of the PNA was difficult at best. The PNA rewarded its elite governing officials with perquisites such as expansive villas and expensive cars. It maintained loyalty in the civic sector by extending its patronage and aid to certain association leaders and members. Many association leaders realized that they could not maintain their social status or obtain the necessary resources for their associations without close links to the PNA. Although many viewed the PNA as corrupt, a far greater percentage of PNA supporters attached prestige to the officials and offices of the PNA. To mingle, associate, and converse with the PNA, as to serve it, bolstered one's personal standing in society as a whole.

When I visited a local youth and sports club in the outskirts of Ramallah, I observed this phenomenon firsthand. My interview with the leader of the association was delayed; he had just returned from a visit in which association leaders were invited to meet and have lunch with President Arafat. The exuberant leader strode into the club with pictures of himself and Arafat, and walked around the association showing the pictures to members and colleagues. As they stared at the pictures with amazement, it was quite apparent that this leader had attained a newfound source of respect and esteem. The leader placed his pictures on the wall for everybody to see. During the course of our interview, he notified me that he had just secured several thousand dollars in aid from Arafat for four members of his club who required medical assistance. Pulling out the authorization paperwork for the disbursement of funds, he pointed to Arafat's signature.

This leader and his sports club became part of Arafat's clientelistic network. In fact, the sports club served as a clientelistic gateway, linking constituents to the PNA and obtaining resources for them that they otherwise would have not been able to attain on their own. In return, the

---

[9]Ibid.

association solidified support for Arafat's PNA. Although most every-thing about this association focused on sports—Ping-Pong tables in the lower level, a weight room to the side of the association, and soccer tro-phies standing on the shelves behind the leader's desk—it was much more than simply a sports club. Residents viewed the association, in close proximity to thirty thousand Palestinians, as a community office directly linked to the PNA. Its members could be ensured not only adequate sports programs, since the PNA provided the resources for equipment and facilities, but also access to the government for other needs such as health care or even employment. As this leader went on to say, "We refer people to get employed in the PNA security services. And we are able to get people jobs."[10]

Association members who supported the PNA repeatedly told me of their connections with and access to the PNA. They derived stature from it and were held in high regard by members of both their associations and the community at large. One leader of a women's association—an asso-ciation that allocated a significant amount of its programs to welfare pro-visions for those in need—said, in a matter-of-fact way, "Of course, we have personal relations with government officials. We are not far away from government. We take any problem we have to the PNA; they listen and they deliver."[11] These associations were able to obtain services for citizens more efficiently than government offices. For many association leaders in good standing with the PNA, this was simply the way things worked. The association leaders who had penetrated and navigated these patron-client circles tended not to see themselves as aiding an authori-tarian project but rather as providing essential assistance to their mem-bers. If they did not take advantage of existing opportunities, hundreds of others would. As another leader stated, "We received some monetary help for our organization from the PNA. I do have some connections. . . . In the Palestinian situation to have these connections in government is very important."[12]

Close access to government channels brought a sense of reassurance and security.[13] Asked what she would do if a government office did not deliver the services it had promised, one leader responded, "If there is any problem, we go to the PNA and solve it. It's a mutual relationship, and I have my personal connections in the PNA. So it's very easy for me to discuss any issue. This serves us well."[14] In fact, a leading representa-

[10]Amaney Jamal, interview with pro-PNA association leader AMA, 1999.

[11]Amaney Jamal, interview with pro-PNA association leader AWS, 1999.

[12]Amaney Jamal, interview with BLH, 1999.

[13]See Tilly, *From Mobilization to Revolution,* for his specification of brokers as centers of power in his model of the polity.

[14]Amaney Jamal, interview with CWA, 1999.

tive in the Ministry of the Interior in Ramallah explained that associations that cooperate with the PNA are assured "protection."[15] These forms of clientelism are pragmatic survival strategies. Since citizens on the margins have limited access to formal institutions, such networks offer a practical means of finding solutions to everyday concerns.[16]

But how did associations less sympathetic to the PNA, or even antagonistic to the PNA, derive protection, security, and government access? Compare the reassured responses from pro-PNA civic leaders with this one from an anti-PNA association leader who, when asked what he would do if a government office denied his association a service it had promised, replied, "We will do nothing."[17] Those associations that actively worked toward democratic reform, rejected corruption and clientelism, censured the PNA, and professed opposing political viewpoints acquired little or no government reassurance, protection, or security. Many professed to be appalled at what they saw as the increasing levels of clientelism and corruption. One association leader, who vehemently criticized not only the PNA but also those who exploited their clientelistic ties, cried foul: "When you see the behavior of the PNA in the economic, social, and political spheres it simply has to do with their poor ethics and mores. Now everybody is stealing, using bribes, and trying to find connections. This is all bad."[18] Another leader of an association unsympathetic to the PNA angrily recalled that though his sports club was promised free T-shirts by the Ministry of Youth and Sports, "They did not give us anything."[19]

Ideologically, some were not willing to compromise their worldview for compensation: "We will accept money without any political regulation, because we refuse any political conditions."[20] Support for both democratic initiatives and individual political inclinations, as well as resentment of the corruption and clientelism that characterized the PNA, cost anti-PNA associations a heavy price: "There are no factories. There are no jobs. Everybody works for the PNA, and is part of the police force. We used to be occupied by one power, *now* we are occupied by two."[21]

Some association leaders were bitter toward the PNA not on ideological grounds but on the grounds that they, too, should have been able to access these clientelistic networks and reap some of the rewards. They

[15] Amaney Jamal, interview with official representative in the Ministry of the Interior, Ramallah, 1999.

[16] See Auyero, "'From the Client's Point(s) of View,'" for a discussion on the ways clientelism is perceived from the viewpoint of clients.

[17] Amaney Jamal, interview with HAM, 1999.

[18] Amaney Jamal, interview with NB, 1999.

[19] Amaney Jamal, interview with DHEL, 1999.

[20] Ibid.

[21] Amaney Jamal, interview with NB, 1999.

saw themselves as potential supporters of the PNA but were angry that the PNA had not responded to either their needs or their wishes to be considered part of the pro-PNA contingent. Explaining that her association was in great need of funds—her association's rent was 110 Jordanian dinars per month—one leader, who identified herself as a former Arafat supporter, recounted her frustration with the lack of reciprocation from the PNA: "We try to coordinate all our programs with the Ministry of Social Affairs. We always show them our proposals and share our project information with them. We don't do anything without first obtaining their permission. Yet, they have not helped us pay our rent."[22] Such competition in the civic sphere over PNA patronage left some association leaders bitter and resentful when they were unable to succeed in penetrating the pro-PNA civic circles.

Although factionalism was a strong determinant of allegiance or opposition to the PNA, it was not the sole factor. Not all associations were staunch ideological supporters of the PNA or avid, dogmatic dissenters. In fact, most associations formulated their affinity with or disdain of the PNA according to a confluence of factors closely intertwined with the aftermath of Oslo and the creation of the PNA. Nevertheless, factionalism was an important part of Palestinian civic life.[23]

FACTIONALISM

Fatah supporters long buttressed Yasir Arafat and his aspirations for Palestinian statehood, and pro-Fatah associations benefited greatly from Arafat's return. Members of Fatah viewed themselves as the vanguard that shielded Arafat from oppositional criticism, mobilizing to demonstrate allegiance to the PNA and competing with anti-PNA forces. Arafat generously appointed his Fatah supporters to key positions in his ministries and posts in his bureaucracy, and, more importantly, he further saturated his security and police forces with Fatah supporters, augmenting support among Fatah followers.[24] By bolstering the role of Fatah in all facets of Palestinian society, Arafat also created a privileged space for pro-Fatah associations. In the end, these pro-PNA Fatah supporters had much more clout in the civic scene than their dissenting counterparts.

Leftist factions and Hamas did not compromise their ideological stances during the Oslo Peace Process and thus found themselves politically marginalized post-Oslo. The leftist parties, for example, were appalled

[22]Amaney Jamal, interview with NAR, 1999.
[23]Tamari, "Palestinian Social Transformation."
[24]Usher, *Palestine in Crisis;* Hilal, "State-Society Dynamics under the PNA."

with the Accords' vagueness and the sluggish progress of the negotiations that would determine the outcome of Palestinian statehood. They demanded an immediate Israeli recognition of a Palestinian state. They had little faith that Arafat could obtain meaningful concessions from Israel, and worried—prophetically—that he would become too enamored of his new status as nation leader to focus on the pressing issues facing Palestinians. Many believed that while Oslo legitimated Arafat as a leader, it did little for Palestinian statehood. Supporters of Hamas disagreed not only with Oslo as a negotiating platform but also with its goals altogether. Hamas refused to recognize Israel's right to exist.

The Palestinian leftists had not yet put forth a viable proposal for a two-state solution and were unable to formulate a strategy to address the Oslo Peace Process.[25] Therefore, many members of the opposition did not participate in the PLC elections of 1996, and although many of the leaders of the former Left sought to establish their own donor-funded organizations, their constituencies became seriously detached from the formal political process. Realizing that the oppositional leadership had practically dissipated, leftist supporters clung to their former politicized associations as the only viable outlets for political expression and representation. These leftist factions remained skeptical of the ongoing peace process, but they were also strong supporters of democratic institutions of governance. They realized that, as opposition movements, they had little chance of partaking in the political process if democratic reforms were not implemented.

As one leader of an anti-PNA association passionately put it, "Human rights are not available!" He went on to state,

> Our freedoms are limited. We have no freedom of the press. We cannot express our opinions. The PNA goes into universities to arrest students and this is against democracy. There needs to be due process. Students have been in prison for four to five years because of their opposition to the PNA. The PNA does not want any competition.[26]

This leader was committed to a democratic framework because only with the freedoms associated with democracy would he be able to freely engage in political society.

Some Palestinian citizens were not members of the opposition but still considered themselves anti-PNA because of corruption and clientelism. These individuals, like members of opposition factions, believed that a

---

[25]Since Oslo, different programmatic and strategic initiatives to recognize Israel have been proposed by both leftists and Islamists; however, these proposals do not proceed from a belief that the Oslo framework will guarantee Palestinians a viable, contiguous state.

[26]Amaney Jamal, interview with KPL, 1999.

true democratic government would safeguard the interests of all citizens. They identified ideologically with a democratic vision of governance and wanted to see the PNA make significant steps toward democratic reform. Their opposition to the PNA was not based on a dislike for Arafat or his Fatah party but rather on a dislike for the PNA's tactics. They feared that the PNA would at best continue to use the language of democracy with no real democratic concessions and, at worst, establish and institutionalize a long-standing centralized authoritarian regime like those in other areas of the Middle East.

Another dimension of associational support for the PNA stemmed from the Palestinian conviction that no leader other than Arafat could deliver a satisfactory peace treaty with Israel. Although these citizens were not Fatah supporters per se, they threw their support behind the PNA to increase its credibility as a governing institution so that it did not appear a weak negotiator with Israel. This contingency saw Arafat as a noble leader who embodied the Palestinian quest to end Israeli Occupation. Without Arafat, they believed, Palestinian hopes would receive a serious a blow. While others may have seen the PNA as abusing its power, these supporters lamented the paucity of viable alternatives; hence, they opted to support what they had in hopes that the PNA would change or bring about democratic reforms. These pragmatically motivated associations were not necessarily strong supporters of the PNA, but they did believe they were better off with it than without it.

Supporters of the PNA were not necessarily antidemocratic, but they were less willing to demand democratic reforms until the PNA was comfortably situated in power. They had faith in the PNA and believed that Arafat would implement democratic reforms once the PNA moved the peace process along. They argued that the PNA was working toward the larger goal of building a democratic state, using its resources to first establish the foundations of a solid state. Therefore, this segment of Palestinian society was unwilling to criticize the PNA. As one such pro-PNA association leader commented, "We cannot expect the PNA to do everything for us. We have to help our state. We, the Palestinian people, expect the PNA to carry a burden it cannot plausibly carry."[27]

Similar sentiments were expressed across the West Bank. Neither Arafat nor his PNA were believed to be inherently antidemocratic; rather, the nature of state building itself was thought to underwrite antidemocratic initiatives. Such associations were consequently less demanding of immediate democratic reforms and were wary of the potentially powerful and disruptive effects of social pressure on the PNA. One PNA sympathizer articulated this vigilant support of the government, saying, "The PNA is

[27]Amaney Jamal, interview with pro-PNA association leader HAN, 1999.

new. The conditions of the PNA are poor. The PNA is trying to get money for itself. We are with it. It is weak. It is *haram* [a sin] to attack it."[28] This Palestinian sector was willing to live with the authoritarian abuses of the PNA—for if the PNA fell, there may well have been no other competent Palestinian leadership.

### THE PEACE PROCESS WITH ISRAEL AND THE REALITIES ASSOCIATED WITH OSLO

Palestinian perceptions of the Oslo Accords in general provided yet another point at which associations divided into pro-PNA and anti-PNA groups. Many Palestinians hoped the Oslo Accords would bring them a final settlement—a true peace treaty—with Israel.[29] Ideologically, supporters of the Oslo Accords were also strong supporters of the PNA. For other Palestinians, to whom Oslo brought nothing but economic misery, further Israeli closures, and dashed expectations, the Oslo Accords advanced the Palestinian cause not at all.

Initially, polarization dipped immediately following the Oslo Accords as the creation of the PNA imparted the semblance of a Palestinian state under formation. But the creation of the PNA also had the effect of introducing new political realities, allegiances, and realignments within the domestic Palestinian front. Palestinian hopes for an imminent, independent statehood were fed both by the Israeli promise to withdraw from the remainder of Palestinian territory in the West Bank and Gaza as well as by Arafat's promise to rule Palestinian society democratically. But as the Israeli Occupation continued and the PNA failed to fulfill its democratic promise, support for the PNA and Oslo gradually fell. Palestinian society grew increasingly polarized along a spectrum of support or opposition to Oslo, a polarization that extended to the associational terrain as well.[30] Within this context, associations found themselves having to renegotiate their political topography and reformulate their civic visions.

While in exile, the PLO had funded the activities of associations tied to particular factions within the PLO as a means of sustaining outlets for political mobilization in the absence of formal Palestinian political institutions. By the late 1980s, aid to the PLO was on the decline. The collapse of the Soviet empire meant that funds and educational scholarships for Palestinians could no longer be guaranteed. Furthermore, Arafat's open support of Saddam Hussein during the Gulf War infuriated many Gulf

---

[28] Amaney Jamal, interview with pro-PNA association leader SSJ, 1999.
[29] Lonning, "Vision and Reality Diverging."
[30] Hilal, *al-Nizam al-Siyasi al-Filastini ba'da Uslu*, 67–70; Salim, *Al-Munathamat.*

leaders who had previously given generous grants to the PLO for disbursement to associations or local charitable societies.

The decline in aid to the PLO during the late 1980s severely damaged Palestinian charitable and local associations, which to this point had depended on securing resources from a variety of sources. Many received funding from the PLO, while Arabs in other countries constituted a significant source of funds for a large number of charitable voluntary associations. Many charitable drives and programs from the Gulf states were designed to help Palestinians. Before 1988, Jordan still claimed legal jurisdiction over Palestinian associational affairs, and it accordingly channeled *Zakat* (Islamic tax) money collected from Jordanian citizens into the West Bank.

But Jordanian disengagement from the West Bank in 1988 and Arafat's support of Iraq drastically decreased the PLO's ability to finance Palestinian civic organization. In 1988, the PLO allocated $350 million to the Territories. In 1990, this figure stood at $120 million, and by 1993 the PLO could scrape together only $40 million. In the space of five years, the PLO decreased its support by some 80 percent.[31] The decline in economic assistance to civic associations from the PLO was directly linked to the dwindling of aid to the PLO from Gulf countries.[32] During the peak of the Intifada, some estimates put PLO financial flows to the Palestinian Territories at $10 million per month, falling to only one-fourth of this amount in 1991.[33]

The beginnings of the Intifada in 1987 also took a heavy toll on Palestinian workers who depended on Israel for their livelihood. Often blocked from accessing Israeli labor markets (as occurred even after Oslo) and thus unable to earn income, Palestinian citizens could no longer continue giving charitable donations to their local community associations.[34] Thus, on the eve of Oslo, the local Palestinian associational terrain desperately awaited new sources of funding. The only viable source was that of the newly created PNA, which received funds from the donor community; however, the differential access of associations to support and aid from the PNA would worsen the polarization that already characterized Palestinian associational life.

The Gulf War demonstrated that a new world order had emerged, an order characterized by US domination of the international scene. The PLO could no longer exploit a bipolar world order in which the USSR gave its open support. Thus, the PLO, on the verge of international alienation,

---

[31]Brynen, *A Very Political Economy,* 48.

[32]Usher, *Palestine in Crisis;* Hilal, *Al-Nizam al-Siyasi al-Filastini Ba'da Uslo.*

[33]*US News and World Report,* 26 Apr. 1993.

[34]Salim, *Al-Munathamat,* for a discussion of local Palestinian charitable contributions and their effects on organizational programs.

found in Oslo an opportunity to map out new relationships with the United States, although the latter, as the sole world power, now had greater leeway to pressure the PLO at the negotiation table. After decades of being shunned by the West as a terrorist organization, the PLO could improve its standing with the Western world by signing the Oslo Accords. A downward spiral in the PLO's popularity in the Territories also pressured the PLO to sign quickly. The Intifada required external financial resources to sustain it, and plummeting Palestinian living standards further increased financial demands on the PLO. The PLO was unable to meet growing Palestinian needs; to the dismay of both Israel and the PLO, rival Hamas began to enjoy the approbation of the Palestinian street. Israel feared that having no other negotiating partner than Hamas would make a negotiated, political settlement to the Palestinian-Israeli conflict impossible.[35]

Whether the Oslo Accords were doomed to failure from the onset is an issue for debate elsewhere, but clearly, specific clashes between Israelis and Palestinians impeded the negotiation process. For Israel, the Oslo Accords should have brought unequivocal security. The major threat to Israel came from the Islamist groups Hamas and Islamic Jihad.[36] In return for recognizing the PNA, Israel expected Arafat to take care of the Islamists and any other oppositional movement that would threaten Israel. This required careful navigation by Arafat. Members of Hamas operated secretly in clandestine cells; so difficult was it to uncover these cells that, before Oslo, even Israel's most sophisticated intelligence units could not locate them. For Arafat to arbitrarily arrest Islamist supporters who were not associated with the military wings of these groups would have undermined his credibility, even among his most dedicated and loyal associates. On the one hand, Arafat needed to maintain his legitimacy as a Palestinian leader safeguarding the interests of the Palestinian people; on the other, he needed to deliver on his promises to Israel.

The Oslo Accords also stipulated that Israel make territorial concessions to the PNA in the West Bank and Gaza. Negotiations dragged on as timetables were delayed and agreements never implemented. Obtaining territorial concessions from Israel that would allow for the creation of a contiguous Palestinian state seemed impossible. Israel's position was that it would not cede territory to the PNA until it was reassured that the PNA had neutralized the Islamists. Arafat claimed that he could not continue to crack down on his own citizens and subject them to interrogations, arrests, and even torture—all of which were making human rights organizations scramble to release reports—without Israel's demonstrating that

---

[35] Usher, *Palestine in Crisis,* 1–13; Hilal, *al-Nizam al-Siyasi al-Filastini ba'da Uslu,* 67–70.

[36] Although Israel had previously turned a blind eye to Hamas's growth in the late 1980s. A stronger Hamas, it was believed, would counter the more secular PLO.

it was committed to a Palestinian state, which would require more territorial concessions and a halt to the building of settlements in the West Bank. In fact, the Oslo period witnessed an increase in the appropriation of West Bank territory for the building of settlements and settlement bypass roads that linked these settlements to Israel even as the number of suicide bombings and other Palestinian attacks increased.[37]

Palestinian attitudes deteriorated in the face of this situation. Some of this deterioration can be directly accounted for by the peace process, such as an increased sense of hopelessness associated with stalled talks, while other matters were indirectly linked to the Oslo process, such as the growing corruption and clientelism marking the PNA.[38] And although the failures of Oslo and the PNA were two different sets of issues, Palestinian assessments of their own situation reflected their dissatisfaction with both. After all, if it were not for Oslo the PNA would not have been created, and Arafat's leadership of the Sulta (Palestinian National Authority) was necessary to the signing of the Oslo agreement, which had been heavily criticized for its vagueness and inadequate mention of Palestinian national aspirations.

Post-Oslo, many Palestinians felt that the sense of community that held Palestinians together during the first Intifada had fragmented. Observers believed that new social developments had created individual incentives, such as recreation and self-promotion, at the expense of communal goals. Even as access to employment was restricted, members of the upper echelons of the Sulta enjoyed luxurious living standards. In fact, many of the newly founded recreation-oriented establishments in Ramallah catered to this new sector of the nouveaux riches. Discos, bars, and ethnic restaurants mushroomed in the city. Jericho established its first casino, but only Israeli citizens, those who carried foreign passports, and those who had received approval from the PNA could enter it. Critics of these establishments included the religious community, which was appalled at the unapologetic flaunting of corrupt practices such as increased alcohol consumption, dancing, and gambling in the Holy Land. Opponents of Arafat

---

[37] The area of West Bank territory appropriated for settlement building increased twofold from 1992 to 1999, from 77 square km to 150 square km. Additional lands were appropriated for bypass roads that in effect divided the West Bank into noncontiguous areas. These roads have restricted Palestinian movement in the West Bank, thereby harming economic and industrial development, commerce, and the movement of labor. The settlement and road building have also prevented the expansion of Palestinian villages and towns and have caused overcrowding in many of these areas. See the Palestine Monitor, http://www.palestinemonitor.org/factsheet/settlement.html, and MIFTAH (Palestinian Initiative for the Promotion of Global Dialogue and Democracy), http://www.miftah.org/Display.cfm?DocId=82&CategoryId=4.

[38] Sourani, "Human Rights Work in Palestine."

accused the PNA of trying to brainwash the Palestinian people into be-
lieving that they had achieved their national aspirations of statehood.
A casino does not a state make, they would argue. These recreational
outlets did nothing more than divert attention from the struggle toward
national liberation—the goal, they claimed, that should be a priority for
every Palestinian.

Supporters of the PNA rejected these claims, arguing that the PNA had
created many jobs. For instance, a card dealer at the casino in Jericho
made over a thousand US dollars a month (not including tips). PNA supporters, however, did not necessarily back all its initiatives. For them, the
post-Oslo Sulta days brought Palestinians the hope of imminent statehood, created new economic opportunities, and ended the violence associated with the first Intifada. For many others, this same period saw the
loss of the Palestinians' sense of national purpose, the worsening of economic conditions, and a feeling of general humiliation.

These mixed conditions and results, directly linked to the Oslo Peace
Process, further fueled the polarization of Palestinian associational life.
Some association leaders have maintained full-fledged commitment to
the PNA even in the face of its growing corrupt practices. One pro-PNA
association leader, who refused to see the PNA as corrupt, argued that
Israel was responsible for promoting this false image of it:

> The corruption in the PNA is due to the Occupation. It is all about the
> Israeli secret services, like the Mossad. They set out to make the PNA
> look bad. Their goal is for the Palestinian people to lose trust in them-
> selves and their leadership. When the Israelis agreed to withdraw, they
> were betting that the Palestinian population within two to three months
> would beg the Israeli authorities to come back and occupy them. One
> way Israel tried to discredit the PNA is that it allowed the spread of il-
> legal weapons all over Palestine. Israel knew that these illegal weapons
> would be used against the PNA. At the same time, Israel did not allow
> the PNA to increase its police forces to control this situation. When the
> PNA tried to arrest those that were making problems, Israel did not
> allow the PNA to arrest them, because it had close ties to these corrupt
> Palestinians. When there were fights in Ramallah, for example, the
> PNA could not control the situation. And when Palestinians were ar-
> rested, they had to be released because the PNA did not have enough
> authority over its own territory to sentence these people. Then Israel
> says to the world that the PNA deliberately allows the spread of illegal
> weapons.[39]

[39] Amaney Jamal, interview with RUB, 1999.

This association leader refused to see any wrongs in the PNA's conduct; he even pointed out Israel's political stakes in perpetuating claims of PNA ineptitude. Although PNA abuses of power were well documented, this leader eloquently spoke of his and others' allegiance to Arafat. These individuals were not only willing to turn a blind eye to Palestinian corruption; they did not even recognize that the PNA was responsible for its own corruption. For many of these leaders, their years of loyalty to Arafat and their view that the PNA embodied Palestinian national aspirations made it difficult even to criticize the PNA.

Other leaders, however, were far more concerned, fearing that the growing levels of corruption were indeed demoralizing Palestinian society. Many association leaders reported that their members had lost faith in voluntary work and the tenets of "good citizenship" after observing the levels of corruption among the ranks of the Sulta. Commented one leader: "Oslo has left us depressed and demoralized. People don't care anymore and are apathetic. After the PNA—people are either very rich or very poor."[40] Another leader concurred: "We are in a situation where things are not clear. The current political situation has hurt us. People do not care for each other anymore. People are not trustworthy. Social work has lost its attractiveness, not like before, because of the economic conditions. People are concerned with money. When we ask people to volunteer, they ask you how much."[41]

Association leaders unsupportive of the PNA also expressed anger and sadness about their inability to provide members with amenities similar to those offered by pro-PNA associations. "Our members used to be willing to pay for projects and services," said one leader. He continued: "Today people say that they will not provide us with much assistance. They tell us that we must provide amenities similar to what the PNA gives its supporters. We cannot afford to offer our members what the PNA offers its supporters."[42] Nor can these anti-PNA associations secure funds from abroad.

## Donor Monies

In the end, the role of the donor community shaped Palestinian polarization in ways that favored Arafat's standing and legitimized both Arafat and his supporters. On the one hand, donor aid further reinforced support for Arafat's PNA. The donor community wanted to see that the Oslo

---

[40] Amaney Jamal, interview with KJS, 1999.
[41] Amaney Jamal, interview with KSM, 1999.
[42] Amaney Jamal, interview with HJD, 1999.

Accords resulted in a final negotiated peace settlement, and it also sought to ensure that the PNA governed democratically. But Palestinians perceived the donor community as "bullying" Arafat into democratic reforms while ignoring Israeli abuses of Oslo—as Israel continued its military occupation and settlement of the Territories. Palestinians decided that the donor community was consistently undermining the PNA in the face of its arduous negotiations. At the same time, the perception—encouraged by the PNA—that the donor community had hijacked Palestinian national discourse silenced some Palestinian dissenters and critics of the PNA. Many felt that donors were all too ready to fund critics of the PNA but did little to scrutinize Israeli military occupation tactics.[43]

The Palestinians who became gradually more skeptical of the donor community argued that they were still in a resistance struggle with Israel; the PNA's democratic accountability should come later. While many who expressed these opinions were often strong supporters of the PNA, even the PNA's less enthusiastic supporters were not willing to blame it for post-Oslo ills. If the Oslo Accords would not meet Palestinian national aspirations, then the donor community had no right to pressure the PNA to become more democratic. Because the PNA was not representing Palestinian national interests through its Oslo negotiations, the donor community should first try to create a better peace settlement for the Palestinians before calling for democratic reform. George Giacaman captures these sentiments well: "To admonish the [PNA] to respect human rights and to govern democratically, without reference to Palestinian national rights and to the failings of the current political process," he says, "is to pay lip-service to those causes."[44] In effect, this increased Arafat's legitimacy and credibility. Further, anti-PNA associations were less willing to resort to donor funds if donors required unqualified support for Oslo. To oppose the PNA without donor support still carried a semblance of domestic authenticity that foreign sponsorship watered down. Anti-PNA associations lacked funding through both the PNA and foreign donors. Even when they could approach the more "neutral" donor agencies, many Palestinian local associations did not possess the expertise necessary to attract donor money effectively.

The most serious confrontations took place between the PNA and the PNGO (the Palestinian Non-Governmental Organizations, created in 1993)—a network of predominately Western-funded organizations working on issues of democracy, development, and human rights. The tension between PNGO and the PNA revolved around three major

[43]Jad, Johnson, and Giacaman, "Transit Citizens," 139; Lonning, "Vision and Reality Diverging," 13; Nimer, *Green Left Weekly.*
[44]Giacaman, "In the Throes of Oslo," 13.

points: funding, licensing, and participation in policy formulation.[45] The PNA often competed with the NGO sector for the same foreign funds. According to Rema Hammami, after eyeing the World Bank's $15 million Palestinian NGO fund, the PNA launched a campaign to rein in Palestinian NGOs, discredit their activities, and limit access to NGO funds in general, estimated at around $100 million altogether.[46] Not only did these strategies divert money away from the NGO sector; they also effectively established many NGOs competing for the same donor money.[47]

When Arafat attempted to consolidate all associational licensing requirements through his Ministry of the Interior (Security Apparatus), the PNGO and other associations raised strong objections, arguing that the PNA would use this ministry to monitor and limit NGO activities. The first draft of the Law of Associations to call for these licensing procedures went further, demanding that the minister of the interior consent to all associational activities. Hence, the Law of Associations was dubbed the "Law of the Minister." Debates ensued in the PLC, and several drafts of the Law of Associations underwent critical evaluative readings. In May 1999 the legislature sent a draft to Arafat for ratification that allowed NGOs to register with the less partial Ministry of Justice, but he returned it with an amendment: the Ministry of the Interior would be in charge of all associational licensing.

This was merely one of the defeats the anti-PNA associational sector aligned to Arafat experienced after the Oslo Accords. The consequent battles between the PNA and the Western-funded NGO sector dramatically unfolded in daily newspapers. The PNA attempted to garner more national support for its methods of rule by accusing these Western-funded NGOs of undermining the Palestinian national project. Abu Meiden, the Palestinian minister of justice, argued that these donor-funded organizations disapproved of the Law of Associations because they did not want to be held financially accountable; millions in donor money, he said, had been squandered by these organizations, for they had done little to meet Palestinian aspirations of development. He described Palestinian NGOs as "fat cats whose job is to distort and discredit the Palestinian Authority."[48]

Palestinian donor-funded organizational leaders responded. Dr. Ghassan al-Khatib wrote in a local ad circulated to many local newspapers that "the tension" between "the PNA and the NGOs is not new." He continued:

[45]Frisch and Hofnung, "State Formation and International Aid."

[46]Hammami, "Palestinian NGOs since Oslo," 16–19, 27, 48.

[47]World Bank sources indicate that funding to the Palestinian NGO sector decreased by 66% during the period 1994–97.

[48]Amaney Jamal, interview with MENL, 14 June 1999.

Put simply, the existence of financially independent organizations whether in development or human rights, contradicts the style of government that the Palestinian National Authority would like to maintain. If the PNA had its way, all active parties or groups and even persons would be dependent, mainly financially, on the PNA. This dependency would be manipulated in order to consolidate the PNA's political power. . . . Therefore, the source of this recent problem is that NGOs are financed directly and independently by the international community in a way that bypasses the PNA and makes them independent. This makes the PNA very nervous.

The NGO sector felt that Arafat would continue to exploit the relationship between the NGOs and their donors to undermine their work.

The most significant threat to Arafat's domestic rule came from this donor-supported civic sector and from Hamas.[49] Hamas vowed to harm the peace process because it viewed the peace process as a complete and embarrassing surrender of land and rights to Israel. The civic sector could also create a voice of dissent and criticism targeted at the PNA, a voice that could potentially discredit Arafat and his authority altogether. Therefore, part of Arafat's strategy of consolidating his power base included maintaining and extending his influence within the civic sector so that no single, unified voice against his support could emerge.

After Oslo, donors almost exclusively funded associations and projects that were linked to or supportive of the goals of the Accords. Those who did not wholeheartedly support Oslo found it difficult to solicit funds. With a lack of access to the PNA and severed or limited ties to the Arab world, these associations were struggling just to stay afloat. Further, the donor agencies had specific agendas and programs of their own that local charitable organizations had difficulty implementing, such as basic grant-writing techniques and language requirements. Donor groups often required that the charitable organizations adopt some of their programs to be eligible for funding. Asked how his association supported itself, one anti-PNA leader reported, "We depend on ourselves. We have financial problems as opposed to other associations who support and get resources from the PNA. And they also get money from outside because they support Oslo. We, and the Islamic associations, don't support Oslo, and therefore it's harder for us to get funding."[50] A leader of an Islamic charitable association agreed: "No, we are not financed sufficiently. Foreign donors tell us to change our names from 'Islam' and they will give us money. Why? There are Christian-named organizations, and they obtain Western funding."

[49] Abu 'Amr, *Al-Mujtama.*
[50] Amaney Jamal, interview with MAK, 1999.

Having faced the prospect of losing her association because of her inability to pay the monthly rent for the worn-down center she occupied, one leader realized that she had no alternative to seeking the financial help of the PNA: "The PNA now gives us money," she said. "It pays our rent. The owner of the building was going to kick us out. Then the head of the Ministry of Finance gave us money. We wrote so many letters and contacted so many people in the PNA. We sent our secretary to the ministry and told her to stay there until the ministry gave her money."[51] This leader was not an ideological supporter of the PNA; in fact, she explained that she was more sympathetic to Muslim groups.[52] In the face of adverse economic conditions, however, she felt compelled to resort to the PNA and defended it, claiming that the PNA would do more to help associations if it had sufficient resources. She also chastised Palestinian society for not paying taxes to the PNA on time: "Palestinians have no problems paying their taxes to the Israelis, but try to avoid paying their taxes to the PNA."[53]

Most donor projects aimed to secure one objective—the success of the peace process with Israel. They aimed at strengthening the institutions of the PNA so that it could effectively and successfully negotiate with Israel. More importantly, donor funding was intended to support the PNA so that it would have the institutionalized ability to crack down on Palestinian oppositional forces that posed security threats to Israel.[54] Donor aid enabled the PNA to build the necessary infrastructure for its offices, pay its employees, establish its own telephone and electricity companies, and create many new investment ventures, such as the industrial parks that were to border Israel. On the other hand, donor monies also made it possible for Arafat to establish his tightly knit network of patron-client relations. "The paradox of (donor-supported) Palestinian NGOs criticizing (donor-encouraged) [PNA] security measures," argues Rex Brynen,

> underscored the dilemmas of this entire sector. The maintenance of security was a fundamental part of any Palestinian-Israeli peace treaty.

[51] Amaney Jamal, interview with INJ, 1999.

[52] Two of the three Islamist associations in my sample were more democratic than pro-PNA associations. This might raise concerns about the "democratic orientation" of anti-PNA associations more broadly. Whether Islamists are democrats for democracy's sake or for purposes of opposition is an ongoing debate in the field of Middle East studies. Nevertheless, recent studies demonstrate there is little reason to doubt the democratic intentions and orientations of Islamist movements. In several parts of the Arab world, Islamist movements continue to champion democratic reforms. See works listed in the bibliography by Ellen Lust-Okar and Jillian Schwedler and Glenn Robinson.

[53] See Roy, "The Transformation of Islamic NGOs," for a discussion on donor funding to Palestinian Islamic associations.

[54] Qamhawi, "Wa-al-Tahadiyat fi Wajh Masirat al-Mujtama' al-Madani," 95; Julia Pitner, "NGOs Dilemmas."

Although not all security measures involved human rights abuses, it was almost inevitable that any crackdown against radicals by the P[N]A would involve a substantial number of excesses. At the same time, donors repeatedly emphasized the importance of human rights and democratic development.[55]

In some ways then the goals of the donor community were at odds.

The dual role played by the funding community further extended the gap between pro- and anti-PNA associations. Arafat's PNA grew in institutional strength and in manpower under Oslo, as did his own ability to further consolidate and centralize his powers.[56] The pro-democracy and pro–human rights donor-funded associations carried on with their discourse of democratic rights and reform. The PNA, a recipient of Western funds, accused the human rights and democracy associations of complicity with the West to undermine its own rule. According to a leading personality in the Ministry of the Interior, "The increase in aid and the increase in number of these Western-funded NGOs is because these NGOs oppose the PNA."[57]

This logical inconsistency is noteworthy. The West had supplied the money to build PNA institutions, to pay the salaries of PNA officers, officials, and security forces, and to construct all the Territories' major infrastructures, such as new roads. That the PNA could then accuse democratic and human rights NGOs of complicity with Western interests was indeed astonishing, given that the West supported both the PNA and Oslo. Although the PNA was itself a project of the West, it strategically chose to confront the United States publicly for its support of Israel, demonstrating that it placed Palestinian interests above those of the United States.

One such example pertains to the Palestine Broadcasting Corporation (PBC). USAID had been funding the PBC with equipment, training, and access to Voice of America programming when it claimed that the PBC was "unhelpful to the peace process, at times inciteful, and at times anti-Semitic."[58] As a result, the United States pulled the plug on its support for the PBC in 1998. The PNA did not alter the programming of the PBC and

[55]Brynen, *A Very Political Economy*, 17.

[56]For a discussion on the effects of donor assistance in Palestine see Anderson, "Peace and Democracy in the Middle East"; Beck, "The External Dimensions of Authoritarian Rule"; Manal Jamal, "After the Peace Processes: Foreign Donor Assistance and the Political Economy of Marginalization in Palestine and El Salvador" (Ph.D. dissertation, McGill University, Spring 2006). Stetter, "Democratization without Democracy?"; Robinson, "The Politics of Legal Reform."

[57]Amaney Jamal, interview with official representative in the Ministry of Interior, Ramallah, 1999.

[58]Brynen, *A Very Political Economy*, 109.

rejected US pressure as a form of complicity with Israel. This incident, like several others, helped the PNA cast doubt on the West's intentions, positioning support for pro–democratic reform and pro–human rights NGOs as attempts to undermine Palestinian national aspirations.

The public dialogue between state and societal actors comforted some observers, who saw this interaction as a sign of pluralism. Others, especially supporters of the PNA, were skeptical. Why were these "foreign-funded" NGOs being so critical of the PNA leadership? Palestinians supportive of the PNA saw these donor-supported pro-democracy and pro–human rights NGOs as Western agents trying to discredit the PNA in the face of tedious Israeli negotiations. Fatah, in support of the PNA, issued a statement condemning the NGO movement, testifying that

> those interested in Israelization and normalization think . . . we need NGOs that are financed by donors who support these developments. . . . These parties and people aim at creating a distorted civil society based on Israeli approval, governed by an elite which is firmly within Israeli control.[59]

For these leaders, democratic accountability meant lending Israel more legitimacy at the expense of Palestinian aspirations.

Another pro-PNA leader argued against donor organizations' attempts to enforce democratic accountability. "In my opinion," this leader argued, "we cannot just ask for things before its time. We are not a state yet. When we talk too much about democracy, it becomes problematic. . . . If you give the opposition too much power it can injure our political cause. . . . And half of our funding goes to democracy NGOs. This is ridiculous! . . . All they say is democracy, democracy, democracy! We need to work together without being loud. So we can all benefit. But if we attack each other, we hurt each other."[60] Significantly, an anti-PNA leader agreed. Like the pro-PNA leader, she too felt that the millions of dollars channeled into democracy initiatives were not being put to beneficial use:

> It is sad. The PNA is not performing well and now we have all these NGOs that take tons of money. Millions of dollars were put into the workshops under "Teaching Democracy." I do not know what the returns are on such initiatives. Tons of workshops to teach us democracy, as if we are a stupid people. . . . How can I talk about freedom for women and I don't have freedom? In the PNA areas, there is no rule of law. There is corruption. Everything is chaotic. They [the funding organizations] want us to say this, but don't want us to address the Occu-

[59]As reported by Middle East Newsline, 14 July 1999.
[60]Amaney Jamal, interview with CSWA, 1999.

pation. I don't think the PNA should be our priority, to have us bump up against each other. The Occupation is our priority now. They [Israelis] are still taking our lands and building settlements. The funding organizations want to divert our attention away from the occupation.[61]

Although she criticized the PNA for its blatant abuses of power, she also feared that the donor-dictated democracy initiatives were attempting to alter Palestinian national aspirations.

None of the donor programs were aimed at addressing the Israeli Occupation or the political difficulties caused by that Occupation. This leader maintained that, in more ways than one, the donor community turned a blind eye to the role the Israeli Occupation had played in hindering economic development and democratic reform. Because she was ambivalent about Oslo and its prospects, as well as the role of donor aid, she was also skeptical about the character of the PNA. Her dissatisfaction with the PNA stemmed not only from its corruption but also from its ties to donor groups that wished to change the Palestinian national imperative. This complicity effectively changed the topic of discussion from a Palestinian discourse based on national liberation to one that tried to squeeze democratic concessions from a government that had jurisdiction over no more than 18% of its nominal territory.

Further, pro- and anti-PNA supporters alike felt that too much money was being diverted to these NGOs for programs that did not address concrete and immediate Palestinian needs. In fact, a substantial majority of associational leaders, regardless of their views of the PNA, were not happy with donor policies in the Territories, questioning the usefulness of donor agendas. Some felt that donor agendas were far removed from actual realities on the ground. "The upsurge in donor funding also created severe imbalances in the resources and programs [for example] of women's groups, as donor interest in training and workshops often focused on the 'hot' topics of democracy and citizenship . . . some [of these projects were] productive, and others [were] activity for activity's sake."[62] One PNA supporter, for example, felt that donor-sponsored programs did nothing to benefit Palestinians while "real" civic associations—associations that, by implication, did—were not receiving aid:

> We have not been getting any money. These [referring to her NGO] are the civil society organizations! Because those other organizations can write "one" word in English, outside donors give them millions! . . . They spent millions of dollars just to discuss issues [referring to "awareness-

[61]Amaney Jamal, interview with NDJ, summer 1999.
[62]Jad, Johnson, and Giacaman, "Transit Citizens."

raising" workshops]. We can all advise and criticize. This is not right! As a charitable organization, what we are doing is better than what they are doing.[63]

Another anti-PNA leader was appalled by donor-supported initiatives in the West Bank that disingenuously adopted a platform of gender equality and democracy. Although donors funded a domestic hotline network, most of the villages did not have phones. Clearly, a fundamental disjunction existed between the ideological initiatives supported by democratic NGOs and the material realities of the Palestinian people. The leader added: "We applied for a practical plan to assist refugee camps, to build sewage systems, and what not. It was refused. If it were a 'democracy and human rights' initiative, we would have been funded. This is all to convince us that we have a government and we need to respond to it, and to convince us that we do not have a larger goal of fighting the Occupation."[64] In many ways, Palestinians viewed donor programs aimed at establishing democracy as an extension of Western colonialism, intended to dictate the national discourse and civic priorities of Palestinian society. Effectually, donor monies either bolstered support for the PNA or at the very least muffled the voices of its critics, which in turn benefited the PNA.

Some members of civic associations threw their support behind Arafat's PNA because they hoped that Oslo would give them a better future. These members did not consider themselves Fatah supporters per se. They may have believed that there was corruption among the ranks of the PNA and may have seen that the PNA as fundamentally undemocratic, but they also felt that the current peace process had brought them the stability needed to increase their professional and human capital.[65] Those who felt that Oslo was kind to them also threw their support behind the PNA, in hopes that the PNA would lead them to better lives.

CONCLUSION

The roots of associational polarization were multifaceted, both including and extending beyond ideological inclinations. Polarization derived from Palestinian perceptions of corruption, democracy, and a better future, as well as economic need and other forms of material necessity. After Oslo, many associations found themselves economically dependent on the PNA,

---

[63] Amaney Jamal, interview with HAN, 1999.
[64] Amaney Jamal, interview with NDJ, 1999.
[65] Rubin, *The Transformation of Palestinian Politics,* 107.

while others were unwilling to compromise their factional loyalties or their disdain for the PNA. They would rather persevere through economic misfortune in anticipation of a true democratic system.

Evaluations of the PNA were intertwined with Palestinian attitudes about the peace process, in which Oslo occupied a crucial position. Some found comfort in the relative stability associated with Oslo, while others saw Oslo as breaking down the communal foundations of Palestinian civic life. Those who worked with the PNA were guaranteed livelihoods, although they were sometimes subsufficient. Palestinian laborers, with restricted access to Israel during the Oslo period, could not secure their day-to-day living expenses; many professed anger with Israel.

Supporters of the PNA also included those who were skeptical of donor assistance in Palestine. Some saw it as a means of undermining the PNA in the eyes of the world. Others saw it as imposing a national discourse that kept attention on the failures of the PNA and off the Israeli Occupation. Still others believed that these donors had no concrete understanding of what donor support should address. Of those associations that were able to attract external funds because they supported the Oslo Peace Process, some saw their new economic ties as a means of resisting PNA authoritarianism, while others saw them as a means of aiding the PNA's state-building efforts. This interplay of this multitude of factors in the end explained opposition and support of the PNA.

In fact, Hamas's electoral victory in 2006 is linked to the PNA's losing its base of support on these multiple dimensions, which include support for Fatah, the peace process, and access to clientelism. The Hamas victory is a direct result of Palestinian dashed expectations vis-à-vis the peace front, growing corruption in the ranks of Fatah and hence the tarnishing of its once noble nationalistic reputation, and the inability of the PNA to continue to finance its clientelistic networks. The forceful rhetoric emanating from the international community, and especially the United States, against the Palestinians during the Oslo period delegitimized the PNA even further. Not only did the rhetorical statements emanating from Washington, DC, play brilliantly to bolster Hamas's standing, but they further chipped away at Fatah's base. Before and after Arafat's death Palestinians saw a very weakened Fatah blamed for Oslo's failure. This further reinforced Palestinians' conviction that US foreign policy was indeed biased against them. To make matters worse, however, Fatah began to be seen as part of the problem and not the solution. While the international community did little to criticize the ongoing harsh realities of the continued Israeli Occupation, the peace process all but in shambles, and the growing corruption in the ranks of Fatah, Palestinian support turned toward Hamas. Fatah increasingly became seen as a sellout (backed by the United States) that would negotiate away Palestinian national aspirations in return for adequate financial aid to sustain its authoritarian grip on Palestinian society. This is how Hamas capitalized on the failures of Oslo.

While the relationship of civic associations to the PNA and to the Oslo agreements was complex, covering many shades of gray, it is clear that associational landscapes were not structured monolithically across contexts and settings. In many developing areas like Palestine, the political polarization of the associational terrain and the dominant role governments play are a fact of life. Associations navigate the contours of their associational environments based on the ways they identify with and situate themselves in terms of key political institutions within that environment. These political realities structure associational behavior differently.

Chapter 4 charts the relationship between associational life and levels of civic engagement in Palestine during the Oslo period, focusing on the impact of polarization on various civic attitudes, such as support for democratic institutions and interpersonal trust. The chapter explores these two dimensions of civic engagement in particular, with specific consideration given to the political context that endowed civic life with meaning.

# CHAPTER FOUR

# Trust, Engagement, and Democracy

IN DEMOCRACIES, civic associations generate higher levels of interpersonal trust, which in turn correlates to democratically oriented community action such as contacting a local representative about a community or personal concern. In countries like the United States, then, civic engagement bolsters democratic participation: people join associations and learn to trust their fellow citizens by engaging with them, which increases their propensity for participating with the local government. But in state-centralized authoritarian settings, higher levels of interpersonal trust do not promote patterns of civic engagement useful to democratic participatory behavior. In these settings, higher levels of interpersonal trust link to support for the authoritarian government.

This chapter finds that in the West Bank civic associations did generate higher levels of interpersonal trust. However, these levels of trust correlated with support for the rule of the PNA. More generally, participation in associations with ties to the parties in power promoted high trust but lower levels of the kinds of attitudes and behaviors important for holding officials accountable, while participation in associations linked to the opposition produced lower levels of trust but a stronger orientation toward democratic values.

This chapter, in addition to examining trust, looks to some other consequences that policy makers and political scientists consider important. Because current works on the democratic skills learned through associational life focus solely on life in democracies, they rarely ask whether associational participation in authoritarian regimes is actually characterized by higher levels of interpersonal trust, higher levels of civic engagement, *and* stronger support for democratic institutions. In the polarized context of the West Bank, while participation in associations did result in higher levels of trust, it did not breed the second-order consequences we commonly expect to find, such as community engagement, political knowledge, civic involvement, and support for democratic institutions. Participation in associations affiliated with the ruling government boosted levels of trust, but, significantly, not other pertinent civic engagement attitudes. In other words, these findings are just the opposite of what one might have expected to find. The results here fly in the face of expectations based on the existing literature on civic associations and democracies.

The far-ranging effects of the simultaneous failure of the Oslo Peace Process and the inception of the authoritarian PNA had polarized associational life in the West Bank, resulting in pro- and anti-PNA associations. Although the reasons that associations supported the PNA varied, the residual effects of that support were similar. These associations enjoyed access that bestowed rights and privileges that anti-PNA associations did not have.

In surveys that did not control for the political affiliations of associations, organization members appeared to display higher levels of interpersonal trust than people who did not participate. For example, an examination of the impact of associational life on levels of interpersonal trust, based on a random sample of 1,200 Palestinians, corroborates what most of the literature on associational life claims (see table 4.1). The expected relationship between participation in voluntary associations and levels of interpersonal trust emerges clearly in some of the polling

TABLE 4.1

OLS[a] Regression Analysis of the Relationship between Association Membership, Demographic Variables, and Levels of Interpersonal Trust among the General Palestinian Population

|  | Interpersonal Trust[b] |
| --- | --- |
| Association member | .126*** |
|  | (.009) |
| Work | .051 |
|  | (.049) |
| Gender | .036 |
|  | (.047) |
| Education | −.068*** |
|  | (.018) |
| Age | .001 |
|  | (.002) |
| Constant | 3.25** |
|  | (.164) |
| $R^2$ | .0205 |
| $N$ | 1,022 |

** Significant at the .05 level.
*** Significant at the .01 level.
[a]With robust standard errors.
[b]See appendix A for operationalization.

data from 1999. During the summer of 1999, the Jerusalem Media and Communications Center carried out interviews with a random sample of 1,200 Palestinians. These data are revealing. We can use an ordinary least squares regression model to assess the effects of associational participation on trust, controlling for pertinent demographic variables such as education, gender, age, and reported employment status. The results suggest that association membership has an independent, positive effect on levels of interpersonal trust.[1]

To understand the real dynamics of associational life, however, one must disaggregate the evidence and look more carefully at the kinds of associations to which people belong. My own survey of 422 associational members in West Bank civic organizations that cut across a wide array of associational and socioeconomic typologies indicates that higher levels of interpersonal trust are inversely related to support for democratic institutions and other important indictors of civic engagement.

### THE POLARIZATION OF PALESTINIAN CIVIL SOCIETY

Studies on the role of associational life in promoting democratic citizenship focus on the roles associations play in creating forums where citizens meet, exchange ideas, and interact with others outside their primary networks. Associations socialize citizens into the patterns of behavior essential for democratic forms of participation. Crucially, this body of literature treats associations as monolithic gateways for more active, responsible, and effective political participation. Such studies assume that, as vehicles for political participation, associations should produce positive externalities—and in this case, civic competency—conducive to democratically effective civic participation. "Associations" become an indivisible category naturally guided by democratic principles of political access, accountability, and representation. But as we have seen, the West Bank's civic sector—the space between associations and the ruling government in power—is anything but monolithic. The current polarization of associational life in the West Bank has, in effect, created two different civic spaces: one for those associations that do have political access to the PNA, and another for those that do not.

The degree to which one person trusts others he or she does not personally know depends on the ability of social networks or institutions to sanction those who break agreements.[2] In polarized settings like the West

---

[1] Those less educated are more likely to have higher levels of interpersonal trust as well. Other demographic controls such as age, gender, and employment status are insignificant.

[2] See Offe, "How Can We Trust Our Fellow Citizens?"; 1999; Fukuyama, *Trust;* 1995; Lin, *Social Capital.*

TABLE 4.2

Typology of Associational Life in Clientelistic and Nonclientelistic Associational Terrains

|  | Nonclientelistic Associations | Clientelistic Associations |
|---|---|---|
| Clientelistic terrain | • Trust decreases<br>• Civic engagement increases<br>• Support for democratic institutions higher | • Trust increases<br>• Civic engagement does not increase<br>• Support for democratic institutions lower |
| Nonclientelistic terrain | • Trust increases<br>• Civic engagement increases<br>• Support for democratic institutions (not applicable)[a] | • Trust with like-minded individuals (within association)<br>• Civic engagement does not increase<br>• Support for democratic institutions (not applicable) |

[a]The assumption is that nonclientelistic terrains are already democratic.

Bank, where the associational landscape is part of the clientelistic terrain of the ruling government, not all citizens are created equal. Members of pro-government associations are afforded the reassurance of government representation and security. As such, members of pro-PNA associations were more likely than members of anti-PNA associations to be confident that they could access adequate channels for recourse if their rights were abused. Members of pro-PNA associations were therefore more likely to trust others; this trust, however, did not necessarily correlate with higher levels of civic engagement and strong support for democratic institutions.

In the polarized setting of the West Bank, and under authoritarian rule more generally, pro-government association leaders serve as intermediaries, linking their members to the government in a vertical hierarchy. (For a general typology that highlights the important characteristics of associational life in both clientelistic and nonclientelistic contexts, see table 4.2.) In these associations, levels of interpersonal trust do in fact increase, but this trust is contingent on the guarantee of political access. Under authoritarian rule, vertical connections create a sense of security that increases levels of trust; these processes are not reliant on face-to-face cooperative interaction with other members, as is the case in a democracy's horizontally structured associations. That these levels of interpersonal trust do not map onto levels of civic engagement and support for democratic institutions should not be surprising at all. Higher levels of support for democratic institutions would mean support for institutions that undermine the ruling authoritarian—yet, nonetheless protective and generous—government already in existence.[3]

Similarly, the disjunction between levels of interpersonal trust and levels of civic engagement is also unsurprising. The processes through which interpersonal trust is gained directly shapes levels of civic engagement. If association members can fulfill their needs through the patron-client channels that their associations make available, they have little need to engage in civic life. Where trust is a function of one's personal ability to penetrate clientelistic gateways, rather than the face-to-face interactions structured by horizontal involvement in associations, second-order patterns of civic engagement will differ qualitatively. Further, there are few incentives for civic engagement under authoritarian regimes that limit meaningful civic involvement. For example, if all citizens know that the ruling incumbent will win an election by over 90% of the vote, which is common in many authoritarian settings, the incentive to engage others in discussion and debate about elections is quite low. The trust generated by the horizontal bonds in democracies bodes well for both acquiring knowledge and engaging others concerned with local community. This sort of interpersonal trust allows for more effective forms of civic involvement.

Nonclientelistic associations in clientelistic terrains lack political access. Their leaders are not clients of the government and cannot easily generate resources through patronage. Therefore, their members must work together to achieve communal goals. Horizontal ties dictate civic life within these associations, but these associations do little to promote levels of generalized interpersonal trust. Members learn about the prevailing clientelistic tendencies in society and understand that they are vulnerable, often running the material risk of being shut down. They are fearful and isolated, with few resources and fewer options when these resources expire; neither are they afforded the state protections and services that benefit their clientelistic counterparts. They understand that in the face of patron-client networks, one's word means little.

The appeal to these groups of democratic institutions and their protection of citizens' rights is readily clear. Members of these groups discuss the benefits of democratic institutions and how a democratic order protects citizens' rights. They continue to engage one another in ways that increase their knowledge and awareness of the surrounding community. The more cognizant they are about the benefits of democracy, the stronger their support for democratic institutions. But, given their isolation, their

---

[3] Please see appendixes A and B for operationalization on interpersonal trust. The questions administered capture patterns of generalized trust, and not simply trust among like-minded individuals.

lack of trust is reasonable. Although they exhibit lower levels of interpersonal trust than secure and protected members in clientelistic associations, their support for democratic institutions remains as strong as their levels of civic engagement.

Vertical associations do exist in nonclientelistic (democratic) settings, and include some religious clubs. These associations tend to increase levels of interpersonal trust between like-minded individuals within those networks, through the vertical ties that link members to their leaders. Because these vertical associations exist in democratic settings, club members are not accorded preferential government protections, and cannot resort to clientelistic channels to secure their interests. They can and do, however, depend on their association's leadership to guarantee their rights. Within vertical associations, members feel more secure and trusting within their associational boundaries. This kind of trust does not generate patterns of civic engagement useful for democratic forms of behavior for much the same reason that clientelistic associations in clientelistic settings do not: members have no need to engage in democratic forms of participation. The hierarchy bolsters interpersonal trust but does not generate interactions that carry over into civic life.

.   .   .

If this theory about the differential effects of participation in associations is valid, then one would expect members in pro-PNA associations to possess both higher levels of interpersonal trust and lower levels of civic engagement and support for democratic institutions. Conversely, those members in opposition associations should possess lower levels of interpersonal trust and higher levels of both civic engagement and support for democratic institutions. The data collected as part of this study show exactly the anticipated pattern.

An initial examination of the findings in table 4.1 supports the wealth of scholarly work highlighting the importance of associations in promoting levels of interpersonal trust. That association membership is positively associated with higher levels of trust may lead students and policy makers of civil society to believe that associations *necessarily* produce the positive externalities important for effective civic engagement. If the task of this book were to end here, the reader could easily come to the conclusion that a society with more associations will in fact generate a larger stockpile of trust important for societal cooperation, which in turn will aid democratic projects.

Building a civic community, one would conclude, starts with building associations. Association membership indeed has a positive effect on levels of interpersonal trust.

## Association Membership and Support for the PNA

Palestinian association members held higher levels of interpersonal trust than did nonmembers, but an examination of levels of interpersonal trust that does not account for associations' political affiliations is misleading. For instance, the survey of the 1,200 Palestinians sampled finds that supporters of Fatah and of the Oslo Peace Process also were more likely to have positive evaluations of the PNA. Because I examine high and low levels of support for the PNA, my dependent variable in table 4.3 has two values—0 for low PNA support and 1 for high PNA support. I therefore use logistic regression analysis instead of the ordinary least squares regression that scholars and policy makers are more accustomed to seeing.[4] Again the results here are not surprising; controlling for other demographic variables that include employment status (work), gender,[5] age, and education, Fatah members were always stronger supporters of the PLO and the PNA (table 4.3). In the post-Sulta phase, many Fatah supporters were employed by Arafat in his police and security services, awarded ministerial appointments, and guaranteed continued receipt of awards and perquisites. Association leaders loyal to Fatah were better positioned to maintain and establish strong ties to the PNA. Table 4.3 also demonstrates that supporters of the Oslo Peace Process held stronger positive evaluations of the PNA. The polarization of Palestinian society, which has effectively granted clientelistic access to supporters of the PNA based on factional loyalties and support for the peace process, has bolstered support for the PNA as well.

Thus far, the data indicate that association membership is linked to higher levels of trust. Further, supporters of Oslo and Fatah were more likely to have positive evaluations of the PNA. In fact support for Fatah increased the probability of support for the PNA by 35%.[6] The task now is to examine whether those members in pro-PNA associations held higher levels of interpersonal trust. In order to examine this hypothesis, I disaggregate the survey data into two sets of categories. First, I place all the members of pro-PNA associations into one group ($N = 205$). I then place all members of non-PNA associations into a second category ($N = 194$). To examine whether pro-PNA associational members held higher levels of trust, I perform a simple bivariate cross-tabulation (table 4.4). Indeed, members in PNA-supporting associations were more likely to have higher levels of trust: 46% of members in PNA-supporting associations

[4]OLS estimates (using a nonbinary dependent variable) are similar to the logistic regression results below.

[5]Men were more likely to hold positive evaluations of the PNA.

[6]Predicted probability holding other variables at their means.

TABLE 4.3

Logistic Regression of PNA Evaluation among the Palestinian General Population[a]

|  | Evaluation of the PNA |
| --- | :---: |
| Work | 004 |
|  | (.183) |
| Gender | −.881*** |
|  | (.177) |
| Education | −.151** |
|  | (.072) |
| Age | .002 |
|  | (.007) |
| Support for Fatah | 1.31*** |
|  | (.167) |
| Support for Oslo | .236* |
|  | (.151) |
| Constant | 1.40** |
|  | (.166) |
| Percent predicated correctly | 71% |
| N | 835 |

* Significant at the .10 level.
** Significant at the .05 level.
*** Significant at the .01 level.
*Note:* OLS regression (with a dependent variable for four categories rather than dichotomous variable used here, yields similar results.
[a]With robust standard errors.

TABLE 4.4

Degree of Associational Clientelism and Levels of Interpersonal Trust

|  | Low Interpersonal Trust | High Interpersonal Trust | Total |
| --- | :---: | :---: | :---: |
| Non-PNA-supporting[a] association | 71.28% <br> N = 130 | 28.72% <br> N = 52 | 100.00% <br> N = 182 |
| PNA-supporting association | 53.97% <br> N = 88 | 46.03% <br> N = 75 | 100.00% <br> N = 163 |

*Pearson chi² = 7.1033, PR = 0.008*

[a]Coding for "Non-PNA-supporting association" category derived from open-ended interviews. See coding in appendix.

held higher levels of interpersonal trust, compared with only 29% of members in non-PNA-supporting associations. Membership in pro-regime civic associations was directly linked to higher levels of inter-personal trust.

EXAMINING INTERPERSONAL TRUST AND CIVIC ENGAGEMENT

Although current studies on interpersonal trust—like Putnam's *Making Democracy Work*—do capture intrasocietal variations among social cap-ital, they do not underscore the effects political context has on this vari-ation. Many studies emphasize the role that association "types"[7] play in shaping social capital, but they do not extend their studies to either the associational terrain or the roles associations play within their immediate political environments. The nondemocratic nature of PNA rule under-mined any checks or barriers to clientelism and patronage. The PNA con-tinued to support its clients, granting them special permissions and rights, while denying those basic rights to non-PNA supporters. Arafat and the PNA were above the law and so enjoyed immunity.

The impact associational life had on trust, therefore, was not equally structured. Levels of trust were shaped by the degree of clientelism (sup-port for the PNA) between associations and the PNA (see table 4.4). Fur-ther, and also of no less significance, levels of trust did not corresponded to support for democratic institutions (table 4.5). Associations that served as clientelistic gateways themselves provided the context in which indi-viduals trusted others, yet these associations did little to promote strong support for democratic institutions.

When we use a logistic model to assess the relationship between trust and support for democratic institutions among association members, the results are even more counterintuitive. Because I examine high and low levels of support for democratic institutions, my dependent variable in table 4.5 below has two values—0 for low support and 1 for high sup-port. I therefore use logistic regression analysis, as I do above.[8] Table 4.5 charts the relationship between trust and support for democratic insti-tutions while controlling for pertinent variables such as age, gender, ed-ucation, employment, and the degree of civic involvement. The model specification in table 4.5 is designed to capture the ways interpersonal trust relates to support for democratic institutions. Civic involvement is included in the equation as a control to capture those individuals who are

[7]Such as churches, unions, secondary associations, etc.
[8]Using OLS regression on a multiscaled dependent variable (rather than the dichoto-mous variable here) yields similar and comparable results.

TABLE 4.5

Logistic Regression: The Effects of Interpersonal Trust on Support for Democratic Institutions among Association Members[a]

|  | Support for Democratic Institutions | Probability Change in Support for Democracy |
| --- | --- | --- |
| Civic index | .193 (.151) | |
| Interpersonal trust | −.396** (.226) | Decrease by 21% (unit *increase* in SC) |
| Gender | .537** (.273) | |
| Education | .411** (.202) | |
| Work | .558 (.392) | |
| Age | .017 (.012) | |
| Constant | −2.69*** (.882) | |
| Percent predicted correctly | 72% | |
| N | 258 | |

**Significant at the .05 level.
***Significant at the .01 level.
[a]With robust standard errors.

more active in their associations as well. Men more than women and those more educated were likely to have stronger support for democratic institutions. More importantly, however, even while controlling for civic involvement and participation, the negative relationship between levels of interpersonal trust and support for democratic institutions persisted. Table 4.5 is quite revealing. As levels of interpersonal trust increase, support for democratic institutions decreases. In fact, while holding all the other variables at their means, a unit change in interpersonal trust from low to high leads to a 21% probability decrease in support for democratic institutions.

Scholarly works on interpersonal trust link it to active levels of civic engagement; the more one engages in democratic civic life, the more one

TABLE 4.6
Measuring Interpersonal Trust, Support for Democratic Institutions, and
Civic Engagement

| | Community Engagement | | Political Knowledge | | Civic Involvement | |
|---|---|---|---|---|---|---|
| | Low | High | Low | High | Low | High |
| Low trust | 78.83% | 66.49% | 69.05% | 64.77% | 27.73% | 65.50% |
| | N = 85 | N = 127 | N = 58 | N = 114 | N = 112 | N = 112 |
| High trust | 29.17% | 33.51% | 30.95% | 35.23% | 27.27% | 34.50% |
| | N = 35 | N = 64 | N = 26 | N = 62 | N = 42 | N = 59 |
| | Pearson chi² = 0.6401 PR = 0.424 | | Pearson chi² = 0.4641 Pr = 0.496 | | Pearson chi² = 1.9776 Pr = 0.160 | |

*Note:* No significant relationship between levels of interpersonal trust and civic engagement.

trusts (and vice versa).[9] In the West Bank, higher levels of interpersonal trust did not correspond to higher levels of support for democratic institutions, as seen above. Nor did higher levels of interpersonal trust correspond to indicators of civic engagement such as concern for one's community, political knowledge about events and news in one's surroundings, and the degree of civic involvement (see table 4.6). One would expect that higher levels of trust would bode well for patterns of civic engagement linked to democratic citizenship. None of the relationships, however, between civic engagement indicators and trust were significant. That is, there were no significant differences between high-trusting and low-trusting associational members on these pertinent civic engagement indicators. *In fact, lower levels of trust were linked to higher levels of civic involvement, political knowledge, and concern about one's community.* These findings fit the typology in table 4.2. Members involved in clientelistic associations achieved political access that offered them representation, security, and protection, which increased their levels of interpersonal trust. Association clients also reproduced hierarchical structures within their associations that mirrored the hierarchy outside the association. These structures within the association produced forms of interpersonal trust not compatible with civic engagement. Further, in settings not guided by democratic norms of participation, the incentives remained

[9]For examples, see Inglehart, *Culture Shift;* Almond and Verba, *The Civic Culture;* and Ulsaner, "Democracy and Social Capital."

low for members to collectively seek to engage one another to produce change or derive benefits from the state. Their demands and needs were already met through the patron-client network, so why should they disrupt a satisfying status quo?

For the same reasons offered above, levels of interpersonal trust generated in clientelistic associations did not correspond with levels of support for democratic institutions either, as table 4.5 illustrates. Support for democratic institutions clearly undermined the methods of rule of the PNA, which provided its supporters with access, representation, security, perquisites, and benefits. Democratic reforms could have undermined the very regime that supported the clients. If the PNA were to fall, what form of government would emerge is not clear, and Palestinians have had enough of chaos and Occupation. Sticking with a satisfactory if not ideal situation seemed far better than risking becoming "losers" in a new political order.

Tables 4.7a and b further explore support for democratic institutions and levels of civic engagement as a function of membership in clientelistic (pro-PNA) or nonclientelistic (non-PNA supporting) associations. Members in hierarchically structured clientelistic associations were less supportive of democratic institutions than members in nonclientelistic associations (see table 4.7a). Because nonclientelistic organizations were not linked to the networks of the PNA, their participation was based on horizontally dictated exchanges with other members. As such, the face-to-face interactions in nonclientelistic civic associations increased their levels of civic engagement as well (table 4.7b).

Levels of interpersonal trust remained lower among nonclientelistic association members (table 4.4). These members understood that without the security and protection of the ruling government, and absent legal provisions and norms that guaranteed them basic civic rights, few channels offered them recourse if their relationships of trust were violated. These "democrats" remained isolated within their civic spheres, cognizant of the political realities that shaped their environment. Through their civic involvement, they engaged others about matters that concerned their daily lives. Stronger support for democracy among association members directly corresponded to greater amounts of civic engagement (table 4.7b). Members with a higher appreciation of democracy were also more likely to have greater political knowledge, were more engaged in the civic activities of their associations, and were more likely involved in local community affairs. These democrats were engaged in the everyday life of their communities and associations.

To get things done, they depended on their cooperative relationships with like-minded members rather than clientelistic favoritism. They sustained their associations through intra-associational, horizontally based

TABLE 4.7A
Associational Clientelism and Support for Democratic Institutions

|  | Support for Democratic Institutions | | |
|---|---|---|---|
|  | Low | High | Total |
| Non-PNA-supporting association | 38.98% | 61.02% | 100.00% |
|  | N = 69 | N = 108 | N = 177 |
| PNA-supporting association | 48.17% | 51.83% | 100.00% |
|  | N = 79 | N = 85 | N = 164 |
|  | Pearson chi² = 2.9253, Pr = 0.087 | | |

TABLE 4.7B
Levels of Support for Democratic Institutions and Levels of Civic Engagement

|  | Community Engagement | | Political Knowledge | | Civic Involvement | |
|---|---|---|---|---|---|---|
|  | Low | High | Low | High | Low | High |
| Low support | 47.86% | 37.63% | 52.33% | 37.22% | 50.35% | 38.07% |
|  | N = 56 | N = 73 | N = 45 | N = 67 | N = 72 | N = 71 |
| High support | 52.14% | 63.37% | 47.67% | 62.78% | 49.65% | 61.93% |
|  | N = 61 | N = 121 | N = 41 | N = 113 | N = 67 | N = 109 |
|  | Pearson chi² = 3.1493, Pr = 0.076 | | Pearson chi² = 5.4458, Pr = 0.020 | | Pearson chi² = 4.8401, PR = 0.028 | |

ties; these ties of trust, however, could not be extended beyond the confines of their associations, where society at large was dominated by a different pattern of affairs, one in which clientelism created less engaged yet trusting "winners" at the expense of more engaged and democratic yet skeptical "losers."

## THE ASSOCIATIONAL LANDSCAPE

The polarization in Palestinian civic life played an important role in mediating levels of trust and views about democratic institutions; support for the PNA related to higher levels of interpersonal trust while support for democratic institutions inversely related to levels of interpersonal trust. Overall, association members had higher levels of interpersonal trust than nonassociation members (see table 4.1). Additionally, among association members, levels of trust and support for democratic institutions inversely related (see table 4.5). Members of clientelistic associations that had positive evaluations of the PNA also had higher levels of interpersonal trust.

Because civic engagement is underwritten by the ways members of society process information about their existing environment *and* about how they interact with the existing institutions of that environment, the polarization of Palestinian associational life had created two different civic environments. Chapter 3 highlighted the ways contextual influences shaped associational allegiances in the West Bank; because of the polarization of Palestinian civic life and the lack of democratic institutions, several Palestinian associational sites became centers of allegiance to the PNA. Palestinian associational life was as susceptible to the whims of authoritarian abuses as any other sector of Palestinian society. Associations did not monolithically instill attitudes and patterns of behavior in a contextual vacuum. Rather, the socializing effect associations had on their members was directly structured by the relationship between that association and the ruling PNA. Members in pro-PNA associations were more likely to be PNA supporters themselves. They benefited from access to the PNA, while members in anti-PNA associations found themselves at a comparative disadvantage. More likely to be critical of the PNA, members of these associations were also more in favor of democratic institutions.

Unlike democratic polities, in which civic spaces are more or less characterized by similarly binding contractual and legal provisions, the Palestinian civic arena privileged those groups that favored and backed the government in power. Pro-PNA associations and their members were accorded legitimacy and respect, monetary benefits, and amenities; they secured public spaces, access to government channels, and reassurance in their civic space. Their levels of interpersonal trust were a result of their ability to access clientelistic channels. Anti-PNA associations did not enjoy similar benefits. They were shunned by government institutions, and in the face of dire economic crisis they continued to suffer. Though these organizations had legitimacy in their civic sectors, the PNA and its supporters attempted to discredit them in the larger social and political environment. Members of these organizations felt neither secure nor reassured. They were more likely to be critical of the PNA and less supportive of its methods of rule. They were also more likely to be stronger supporters of democratic institutions—institutions that would guarantee them the security and access they so sorely lacked. Even among Islamist associations, which were anti-PNA, this too was the pattern.

Anti-PNA association members were also more supportive of other features of democracy more broadly. Unlike pro-PNA association members, anti-PNA association members were more likely to believe that corruption was widespread; in 1999, 61.7% of these members who were surveyed reported that governmental corruption was high, compared with only 43.82% of pro-PNA members.[10] Of anti-PNA association members, 90.76% adamantly held the freedom to criticize the government as important, opposed to 71.88% of pro-PNA members. While 42.95% of those sympathetic to the PNA stated that they could criticize the PNA without fear, only 30% of members in anti-PNA associations felt that they could do so. Among PNA supporters, 28.18% of PNA supporters maintained that different political orientations—other than support for the PNA— should not be addressed in the public space, where only 12.17% of anti-PNA members surveyed reported this. Finally, 49.41% of pro-PNA members felt that it should be considered illegal to call for the fall of the PNA; of association members less sympathetic to the PNA, 32.09% advocated the illegality of the expression of such sentiments. That anti-PNA citizens were more likely to be supporters of democratic institutions raises serious doubts about the compatibility of levels of interpersonal trust and support for democratic institutions in the West Bank. Put simply, where there were higher levels interpersonal trust, there were lower levels of support for democratic institutions.

That levels of interpersonal trust were higher among pro-PNA association members might appear perplexing; however, within the context of the West Bank, the link between support for the PNA and interpersonal trust was quite sound. Absent the rule of law and legal institutions that guaranteed and protected citizen rights even as they curbed the abuse of patron-client ties, pro-PNA supporters relied on clientelistic networks to secure their interests. Pro-PNA association members, acknowledging their leaders' ties to the PNA, also felt secure in the knowledge that they had access to a resource that could, when necessary, protect them and help them secure necessary paperwork, much-needed financial help, or other needs.

Trusting your fellow citizens is not necessarily the same as regarding them with less skepticism or suspicion, as conventionally understood in political cultural studies. Rather, trusting your fellow citizens means knowing that if a "stranger" tries to abuse a cooperative relationship, a higher legal order will protect citizens—or at least well-connected citizens—from that abuse. In other words, suspicion, or the lack thereof, need not be the explanatory variable driving trust; instead, we must look toward the availability of institutions that potentially resolve disputes when trust relationships are broken.

In the case of the West Bank, pro-PNA association members were accorded comforting gestures by the government. In the absence of effective

---

[10] This series of classification is based on member attitudes in respective pro- or anti-PNA associations.

democratic institutions, anti-PNA association members could not hold feelings similar to those of pro-PNA members. Being more critical of the PNA by definition, anti-PNA associations and their members navigated a precarious environment. On the one hand, they felt that the pressure for domestic reform needed to come from within, through their own labor and efforts: these were reasons they gave for their civic involvement. On the other hand, these anti-PNA members were confronted by pro-PNA members in a civic sector whose advantageous position vis-à-vis the governing authority facilitated their civic participation. Pro-PNA civic participants enjoyed more public access, legitimacy, visibility, and resources, all of which further encouraged and bolstered their participation. As a result, those critical of the PNA competed not only with pro-PNA associations but also with the PNA itself. As these anti-PNA associations were blocked from active civic participation in society and confined to their own civic sectors, they understood that their only hope for emergence was a government that would institute democratic reforms from above. In this formulation, the distrustful, yet democratically oriented anti-PNA association members carried the impetus needed for democratic reforms. They were supporters of democratic institutions, but their current experiences had left them isolated, shunned, and demoralized, with little faith in the governing institutions surrounding them. As a group under surveillance, they had little faith in society at large; they feared persecutions, they feared ramifications, and they feared undue harassment.

Only within a system of rules and rights, where the rule of law is clearly marked, can citizens depend on a legal process to protect their interests. Democratic institutions protect individual civic rights from abuses by fellow citizens and government powers. Members in anti-PNA associations, who were less trusting than their pro-PNA counterparts, were avid supporters of democratic institutions. Where leaders and members saw the abuses of power, they were more likely to become distrustful; this distrust in turn necessitated the intervention of third-party legal, democratic institutions that could protect citizens' interests. Without democratic institutions that guaranteed their equal existence and participation, they feared they would forever be relegated to the fringes of civic life.

Pro-PNA association members, too, may have supported democratic institutions, but not as enthusiastically as those in the opposition. They may have felt that the PNA was representing their interests *adequately,* albeit in a clientelistic fashion. Hence, they felt that representation was what mattered in a system of governance—and not the actual type of government that emerged. Conversely, they may have felt supporting democratic institutions to be inherently contradictory to their open support for the PNA's authoritarian rule. Both these phenomena explain the lower levels of support for democracy among pro-PNA members.

A NOTE ON SELF-SELECTION AND CAUSALITY

My argument here has thus far examined the role civic associations play in the promotion of democratic attitudes. I find an inverse relationship between trust, on the one hand, and support for democratic institutions and civic engagement indicators, on the other hand, among association members. Further, I have demonstrated that associational access to the PNA mediates these findings. A larger question remains unaddressed in this research project—did people self-select into associations that were pro-PNA or anti-PNA? In other words, did members with preexisting commitments to democracy choose associations that were anti-PNA? Absent data across time, answering these questions is difficult. Considering the wealth of data derived from my participant-observation and open-ended interviews, however, there is little reason to believe that self-selection occurred a priori. Members often joined associations that were close to their places of residence. They joined the association to address immediate priorities: to derive services and benefits, to bolster their human capital, and to serve their nation. Further, while some members may have self-selected into associations based on ideological considerations, the ideology of associations was not static. In other words, after the emergence of the PNA, many associations that would have otherwise been strong ideological supporters of the PNA no longer maintained their ideological affinities to the government. Those associations that received direct support from the PNA and were initially supportive of Fatah, for example, remained strong supporters of the PNA. Yet other associations, committed to Fatah, realized that the PNA was no longer paying attention to them—and they ended up becoming part of the opposition. The relationship with the PNA and the ability of the association to become a client, to a large extent, determined levels of support for the PNA and in return structured the relationship of civic engagement indicators within these associations. Through my examination of associational patterns of engagement with the ruling regime, I found that prior to Oslo several associations did not feel affinity to either Arafat or the PLO. After Oslo, they became supporters of the PNA because the PNA offered financial help and support. Conversely, other associations that had worked for Fatah for decades were no longer supportive of the PNA during this time period because they felt the PNA had turned its back on them. In many ways, the polarization I document in this book is based on the realities linked to the post-Oslo period. Ideological cleavages remained important, but clientelistic access to the PNA became paramount.

Therefore, ideological orientations alone did not explain support for or opposition to the PNA. Some associations that were strong supporters of the PNA remained so after receiving generous support from the regime.

Members joined associations for several reasons. They joined primarily to derive services. Yet it is feasible that some members may have joined based on their ideological convictions. Some members may have opted to join associations that were either supportive or in opposition to the government depending on their orientations or convictions. In the end, this self-selection process is one that I cannot control for in the parameters of this study. What I can say is that given the dynamic and fluctuating environment, *even if* these self-selection processes did take place, they demonstrate that associational life cannot escape the overall polarized political setting within which they operate. The density or number of civic associations will not overcome the existing political polarization on the ground. In fact, my study demonstrates that these civic associations become agents that play into this existing political polarization on the ground.

CONCLUSION

Current studies on the role of interpersonal trust in promoting the kinds of civic engagement useful for democratic outcomes address cases that have been guided by preexisting democratic contexts. Most studies, that is, have been conducted from a perspective that assumes democratic preconditions. Whether higher levels of civic engagement and interpersonal trust lead to stronger democratic outcomes depends on the intervening variable of an inclusively democratic polity. Such a polity not only guarantees citizens' rights but also restricts clientelism and guarantees that corruption and abuses of power are publicly addressed. In these cases, civic engagement reflects the preexisting democratic environment, and civic behavior is predicated on established participatory conduits.[11]

Associations do not emerge and function within a vacuum. Where vertical patron-client relations are embedded in state-society affairs, further exacerbated by preexisting polarization and politicization, there is no reason to believe that the associational terrain will not conform to the environmental dictates. Based on this evidence, one questions the conclusion that civic associations necessarily promote democracy. In the case of the West Bank, the quantity of associations does not appear to be a significant factor in shaping civic attitudes; rather, they are shaped by the nature of

[11]Not all associations in democracies influence members similarly. The content and form of levels of civic engagement in associations in such areas as inner cities and ghettos, where citizens may feel marginalized, oppressed, mistreated, or discriminated against, will be different in content and form from civic engagement in associations that are not constrained in these ways.

associations' ties to the ruling government. An increase in the number of associations in the West Bank will not increase support for democratic institutions, because the existing political environment will segregate these associations into either pro- or anti-PNA camps.

Clearly, context matters. And only after we understand how different contexts affect patterns of interpersonal trust and their relationship to civic engagement will we have a nuanced understanding of the role of civic engagement in democratic reform. Crowning interpersonal trust with benevolent and unequivocally "democratic" residuals may be applicable in democratic settings, but it certainly is not in nondemocratic ones. While the high levels of cooperation fostered by interpersonal trust are useful for the efficiency of democratic institutions, this form of cooperation is also useful to support authoritarian settings. Authoritarian leaders depend on their supporters and followers to cooperate to protect the interests of the state and its rulers. Significantly, the forms of social capital praised in current scholarly discourses as useful for democracy are also useful for authoritarianism.

In this chapter, I demonstrate that not all forms of associational life are useful in promoting the type of interpersonal trust and civic engagement valuable for democracy. I demonstrate that an overall assessment of the democratic functions of civic life needs to be juxtaposed with an examination of other pertinent qualities important for democratization, such as support for democratic institutions. In other words, interpersonal trust as a dimension of social capital on its own, in settings that are nondemocratic, reveals very little about the prospects of patterns of behavior important for democratization. In the next chapter, I extend these arguments to other Arab countries. In chapter 6, I introduce a theory of democratic citizenship in nondemocratic areas.

# CHAPTER FIVE

# Beyond Palestine: Morocco, Jordan, and Egypt

LIKE THE PALESTINIAN National Authority, the Moroccan regime extends a helping hand to followers and supporters. Over the years, the Moroccan regime has woven an intricate web of administrative controls, and it easily manipulates the allocation of power and resources—media access, financial support, political access, legitimacy—to supporters and opposition members in both the political and civil spheres, effectively controlling the organizations that form the foundation of Moroccan civil society. This chapter, in detail, will extend the findings of the Palestinian case to the Moroccan context. Furthermore, this chapter will also discuss, in less detail owing to data limitations, state-society relations in Jordan and Egypt.

The Royal Charter of 1958 and the Royal Decree of November 27, also adopted in 1958, guarantee freedom of association in Morocco. Both laws were amended in 1973 with the "Préalable Déclaration" (DP), which granted the regime more authority to limit the growth of associations and inspect their activities. The Ministry of Interior currently scrutinizes associations' activities, and the process of registering an association is tedious. Often, however, the palace's most effective tool is not the restrictive NGO laws themselves but the application of those laws. All associations need to submit a DP to the appropriate regime agency (typically, each *wilaya*—district—has a special office in charge of registering and overseeing associations). In the DP, leaders and founders must reveal their identities and state the purpose of the organization. The agency then forwards the DP to the proper authorities. Once these government channels acknowledge receipt of the DP, the association can proceed with its licensing process. As one researcher comments, "In theory, the authorities should issue that document automatically upon receipt of the DP. In practice, however, nothing compels this or specifies a time span. Thus, merely by refusing to deliver the document acknowledging submission of the DP, the state can deny an association the formal approval that it needs in order to operate."[1]

By maintaining control over such administrative processes, the monarchy effectively prevents the creation of organizations that it does not approve of. For instance, between 1996 and 1998, authorities refused to

[1]Denoeux, "Morocco's 'Fight against Corruption,'" 5.

legalize Transparency Maroc (TM), an advocacy group that concentrates its activities on fighting corruption in Morocco. Until the mid-1990s, corruption was a taboo subject in public discourse,[2] a subject permissible to discuss only under the guise of unethical behavior.[3] Because of TM's interests in corruption, the regime serially found various reasons to deny its DP. State officials claimed that TM had not filed all the required documentation; another official noted that the authorities had not approved the meeting at which TM was created. Still another suggested that the government had not given its approval to the association's inaugural meeting. Finally, the Ministry of Interior described the ties between TM and Transparency International, the international NGO with which it was linked, as "unclear." Only in January 1998 did the obstruction come to an end. The state had evidently grown tired of the standoff and decided to legalize the association.[4]

The length of the legalization process depends on the regime's willingness to see the association come into existence.[5] Pro-regime associations thus have a much higher likelihood of enjoying legal status. Even after associations acquire legal status, however, the Moroccan regime still uses a variety of tactics to maintain control over them, often coercing them to adopt more pro-regime stances.[6] If they do not conform to regime expectations, the NGOs are often barred from government services and protections, including financial services.[7] Because civil society in Morocco does not yet enjoy wide popular support, it must rely on volunteers from the middle and upper classes and "subsist on private contributions and gifts, which are rare."[8] Through its financial contributions to NGOs, the Moroccan regime influences civil society. As a result, NGOs that have been set up by persons close to the regime continue to enjoy close relationships with the authorities.[9] Today, civic life in Morocco still faces overwhelming regime restrictions.[10]

---

[2]In one of his many examples of the manifestations of the taboo, Denoeux describes with what care one organization avoids using a word in its discussion of the phenomenon. "In December of [1995] . . . , the association *Ribat al-Fath*—one of the so called 'regional associations' created from the mid-1980s onward by individuals close to the Palace—organized a colloquium entitled 'Ethics, Deontology and Growth.' For three consecutive days, participants used the word 'ethics' hundreds of time[s], but not once mentioned 'corruption.'"

[3]Denoeux, "Morocco's 'Fight against Corruption,'" 3.

[4]Ibid., 5.

[5]United Nations Development Program (UNDP), http://www.pogar.org/countries/finances.asp?cid=12; Korany, "Restricted Democratization from Above," 62–63.

[6]Najem, "State Power and Democratization in North Africa."

[7]Korany, "Restricted Democratization from Above."

[8]El-Glaoui, "Contributing to a Culture of Debate in Morocco," 160.

[9]Denoeux, "Morocco's 'Fight against Corruption,'" 5.

[10]Layachi, *State, Society and Democracy in Morocco.*

These machinations mean that the associational landscape in Morocco is polarized along axes of support for and opposition to the regime in power. Despite recent gestures of political liberalization, the Moroccan monarchy remains authoritarian and can exert such control. As in Palestine, associations that are supportive of the regime promote programs and initiatives that mimic regime stances. Associations that are more critical of the regime—those that focus their attention on governmental abuses, documenting the abuse of authority and highlighting the need for democratic reforms—not only receive no support but are actively obstructed. Members of associations that support the regime exhibit higher levels of trust and lower levels of support for democracy. Conversely, members of associations that are less supportive of the regime have lowers levels of trust and higher levels of support for democracy.[11]

## Trust and Associational Life in Morocco

Based on World Values Survey data, controlling for other pertinent demographic factors such as age, gender, and education, associational life in Morocco is directly linked to higher levels of interpersonal trust. Association members are more likely to hold higher levels of interpersonal trust than nonassociation members (see table 5.1).

Yet, as in Palestine, support for democracy is higher among Moroccan association members who have lower levels of interpersonal trust (see table 5.2).[12] Furthermore, levels of political confidence mediate these findings. Those association members with higher levels of political confidence in the Moroccan government have higher levels of trust as well as lower levels of support for democratic institutions than those who have lower levels of political confidence (see tables 5.3a and b). The relationship between trust and support for democracy is again, as in Palestine, the opposite of what one might expect.

[11] The World Values Survey conducted in Morocco does not have data at the association level. Therefore, I am unable to demonstrate the relationship between associational proximity to government and levels of civic engagement of associational members. I use member (and not associational) support for the government as a proxy measure here. I am invoking the assumption that members who are supportive of the government are more likely to be in associations that are supportive of the government as well.

[12] Because I do not have data at the association level (I base this analysis on the World Values Survey question on association membership), I cannot statistically demonstrate the effect of associations' *relationships with government* on levels of civic engagement. What I do here is show that member attitudes about government are directly linked to similar patterns of engagement observed in Palestine. I am invoking the assumption that pro-regime associations are more likely to have members that are pro-regime as well (a pattern observed in Palestine).

TABLE 5.1
Logit Analysis: Trust and Association Membership
in Morocco

|  | Interpersonal Trust[a] |
|---|---|
| Association member | .418*** |
|  | (.126) |
| Gender | .469*** |
|  | (.177) |
| Education | −.116*** |
|  | (.041) |
| Age | .006 |
|  | (.007) |
| Income | .017 |
|  | (.051) |
| Constant | −2.05*** |
|  | (.439) |
| N | 1,205 |
| Percent predicted correctly | 78% |

*** Significant at the .01 level.
[a]See appendix A for operationalization.


TABLE 5.2
Relationship of Interpersonal Trust to Support for Democracy among
Association Members in Morocco[a]

|  | Low Support for Democracy | High Support for Democracy | Total |
|---|---|---|---|
| Low interpersonal trust | 18.46% | 81.54% | 100.00% |
|  | N = 24 | N = 106 | N = 130 |
| High interpersonal trust | 36.00% | 64.00% | 100.00% |
|  | N = 18 | N = 32 | N = 50 |

*Pearson chi² = 6.2093, PR = 0.013*

[a]See appendix for coding.

TABLE 5.3A

Degree of Association Members' Confidence in Government and Levels of Interpersonal Trust[a]

| | Low Interpersonal Trust | High Interpersonal Trust | Total |
|---|---|---|---|
| High political confidence | 65.93% | 34.07% | 100.00% |
| | N = 60 | N = 31 | N = 91 |
| Low political confidence | 80.00% | 20.00% | 100.00% |
| | N = 88 | N = 22 | N = 110 |
| Pearson chi² = 5.0749, Pr = 0.024 | | | |

[a]See appendix for coding.

TABLE 5.3B

Degree of Association Members' Confidence in Government and Levels of Support for Democracy[a]

| | Low Support for Democracy | High Support for Democracy | Total |
|---|---|---|---|
| High political confidence | 18.75% | 81.25% | 100.00% |
| | N = 15 | N = 65 | N = 80 |
| Low political confidence | 28.87% | 71.13% | 100.00% |
| | N = 28 | N = 69 | N = 97 |
| Pearson chi² = 2.4394, Pr = 0.118 | | | |

[a]See appendix for coding. Different questions are used here to gauge support for democracy than are used in chapter 4. The World Values Survey unfortunately did not ask questions similar to those I administered in the West Bank.

Association members with stronger evaluations of the Moroccan regime mirror their pro-PNA Palestinian counterparts. In Morocco, the current regime continues to extend its influence to the associational terrain, rewarding followers, encouraging partnership and compliance, and punishing dissenters—fostering trust and demonstrating why democracy may not appear to be the best alterative for members of regime-supporting associations.

Although the factors that shape Moroccan political polarization are different from those in Palestine (support for the regime, for example, is not structured around the Israeli Occupation), many parallels exist. Clientelism and favoritism both remain salient factors in explaining support for and opposition to the government. And although political cleavages divide the associational terrain, the polarization marking Moroccan civil society is structured around clientelitsic access to the regime. Focus-

ing on such polarization, this chapter first provides a historical overview
of the ways in which the Moroccan regime used its powers to bolster its
standing within the associational landscape. It then illustrates the existing
polarization by providing evidence from interviews of Moroccan association leaders.[13]

## Consolidating the Moroccan Monarchy: A Historical Overview

After independence from the French in 1956, Morocco emerged as a
consolidated monarchy; power rested comfortably within the hands of
the regime when Mohammed V (1956–61) came to power and established
a consultative monarchy. The objective of the Consultative National Assembly was simply to gather key figures, handpicked by the monarchy,
from political parties, associations, and professional groups to serve as a
cabinet of advisers.[14] The assembly garnered no real power, however, and
simply ratified the king's decisions.

Under King Hassan II (1961–99), the monarchy became even more
highly centralized. Hassan II appointed trusted confidants and allies in
key governmental posts to deal with opposition forces. Both Ahmed Rida
Guedira and Driss Basri served as his loyal prime ministers, preventing
any opposition movement from seriously challenging the monarchy.[15]
Morocco faced numerous economic problems under Hassan II, including
growing debt and high unemployment rates (18% among the general
population, 34% among the youth).[16] Under external pressure from the
international community to reform economically and facing internal riots
from opposition to rising prices, Hassan II strategically granted more
powers to the opposition.[17] Instead of promoting democracy, however,
these policies only further secured his rule.

The original Moroccan constitution, written in 1962 by Hassan II, consolidated power completely in the hands of the monarchy. With public
pressure mounting, Hassan II promulgated revised constitutions on three
different occasions, in 1970, 1972, and 1992. Although on each occasion
he sought to alleviate public pressure by granting more power to the opposition, the constitutions ultimately "confirm[ed] the preeminence of
the monarchy and the subordination to it of all other political institutions,

---

[13]Over thirty interviews were conducted with Moroccan association leaders in the fall of
2005 by my research assistant Alexandra Kobishyn.

[14]Korany, "Restricted Democratization from Above," 165.

[15]Howe, *Morocco.*

[16]Denoeux, "Morocco's Economic Prospects," 15–42.

[17]In one decade alone—the 1980s—Moroccans took to the streets on three separate occasions (1981, 1984, 1990). See Korany, "Restricted Democratization from Above," 62–63.

whether legislative, executive or judicial."[18] So although members of the Majlis al Nawab (the assembly) are directly elected, under Hassan II's constitution the king can dissolve parliament, legislate during recess, declare states of emergency, or revise the constitution by submitting amendments to a national referendum. Further, an array of constitutional provisions (articles 45, 46, 55, and 58) allows appointed entities to enact laws or veto decisions emerging from the parliament. Thus, even if a government has direct popular and majority support, as does the directly elected Chamber of Representatives, the Moroccan constitution gives it no guaranteed protection from royal interference and administrative maneuvers.[19] Consequently, the king sees the chamber more as a consultative than a deliberative assembly. The assembly is "expected blindly to support whatever the king proposes, and never challenge those ministers in whom the king has publicly placed his trust."[20] And although parliamentarians are now allowed to criticize the regime and monarchy in open debate, the limits of such freedom are still questionable. Articles 23 and 28 still stipulate that it is a crime even to criticize the king's policies and decisions, and article 39 holds that members of parliament can lose their parliamentary immunity for expressing opinions that may be considered disrespectful to the king. As Maghraoui reminds us, practice is much different from theory: "in practice deputies simply refrain from saying anything that could possibly be construed as *lèse-Majesté* [against the monarch]."[21] From the inception of the Moroccan state, the king has been granted the title "Commander of the Faithful" (article 19). He is a leader with a powerful religious dimension—a quality that, according to Bendourou, "raises the king above other institutions and above any juridical order . . . [allowing him] to limit the sovereignty of the nation insofar as the king is invested with power by the divine will."[22]

The overwhelming concentration of power in the hands of the regime left the assembly, the political parties, and civil society actors with little real input. As one observer noted, from 1961 to 1999 King Hassan II "reigned over Morocco exactly as if he were running a medieval absolutist state";[23] he wanted parliament to remain a rubber-stamp institution without any control over executive authority.[24] Today, the king is responsible for appointing the prime minister and the heads of the powerful "ministries of

[18]Bendourou, "Power and Opposition in Morocco," 110.
[19]Ibid., 79.
[20]Ibid., 111.
[21]Maghraoui, "Monoply and Political Reform," 79.
[22]Bendourou, "Power and Opposition in Morocco," 110.
[23]Maghraoui, "Political Authority in Crisis."
[24]Korany, "Restricted Democratization from Above," 62–63.

sovereignty," which include Justice, Defense, Foreign Affairs, Religious Affairs, and the Interior; this last ministry is responsible for security services and the licensing of civic associations and political parties and also oversees both regional and local budgets. The king fills most local government and nongovernment positions, including "governors, prefects of economic regions, heads of administrative provinces, secretaries of state in each ministry, directors of public agencies and enterprises, and judges and magistrates, as well as half of the members of the High Constitutional Council, including its president."[25] Thus, administrative control of both the country's purse strings and its bureaucratic functions rests exclusively within the king's sphere of influence. Since the king needs no additional approval of his nominations, he always grants these positions—especially the minister of the interior—to strong supporters of the monarchy.

The regime has also used informal tactics of clientelism and corruption. The system that the regime co-opts, the *makhzen,* has been for three centuries a vital institution in the everyday management of Moroccan political affairs. According to Bahgat Korany, the word refers literally to "the warehouse where goods and provisions are stored. In Morocco's political context, specialists use it to denote government as a network of power and grants from the top rather than balance and mutual concessions among the different organs."[26] The monarchy is clearly in control; it rules through arbitration and the distribution of rewards. To bolster this royal monopoly, the palace has revived past practices of promoting a well-developed clientelistic system of administrators and politicians.[27]

Hassan II strengthened the *makhzen*'s manifestation as a premier institution of clientelistic gifting. Rewarding his close allies and collaborators, he "distributed high administrative and government positions, immense state-subsidized benefits and services and hundreds of farms and companies recovered from the French in the early 1970s."[28] The beneficiaries of the *makhzen* are called *khadims*—the king's personal servants. In return for their service, *khadims* become the primary purveyors of centralized authoritarian power. The ideal *khadim* is both loyal and discreet. Discretion implies that the *khadim* neither outperforms the heroic deeds of the king nor flaunts his material wealth publicly in ways that embarrass the regime. And although the *khadim* does engage in corrupt dealings, he should be careful not to leave a trace. The daily machinations of the *makhzen* have raised questions about corruption among an increasingly disgruntled Moroccan society and have fed the polarization that characterizes

[25]Maghraoui, "Monarchy and Political Reform in Morocco," 79.
[26]Korany, "Restricted Democratization from Above."
[27]Ibid.
[28]Maghraoui, "Monarchy and Political Reform in Morocco," 79.

state-society relations. In the mid-1990s, after a World Bank report highlighted the levels of corruption in Morocco, Hassan II himself initiated anticorruption campaigns. Widespread financial fraud and embezzlement permeated a variety of government sectors, including banking, social security, agricultural credits, public housing, state contracts, public companies, municipal councils, and international aid projects. Seldom, however, were corrupt senior officials held accountable.[29]

Hasan II also appeased numerous dissenters through co-optation. The multiparty electoral system in Morocco in effect has operated as a tool to select and control a dependent political elite.[30] Through quota systems to balance parties, the bribing of thousands of voters, and the promotion of clientelism, Hassan II protected his rule.[31] All in all, the traditional foundations of centralized monarchical rule in Morocco—despite years of political liberalization—are still intact. Today, the Moroccan monarchy is still the chief patron and ensures its longevity by maintaining a strong, loyal base.

## SOLIDIFYING AUTHORITARIANISM OR POLITICAL LIBERALIZATION

Beginning in the mid-1980s into the 1990s, Morocco witnessed some of the greatest levels of political liberalization among Arab countries. Mohammed VI's accession to the throne in 1999 defined a new vision for Morocco, one with less toleration of human rights abuses and more political and civic freedoms. These liberalization policies granted civil society organizations much more latitude and freedom. The king also held fair elections and limited the engrained pattern of corruption at the polls. Mohammad VI introduced a system of proportional representation where citizens cast their votes for parties to prevent vote buying for individual candidates; he instituted the development of a new ballot that displayed the logos of political parties to enable the illiterate to vote on their own. Voters must now dip their thumbs in ink to prevent repeat voting.[32]

As a result of these changes, some observers have called the 2002 election the fairest and freest election in Morocco's history. Mohammed VI also dismissed Driss Basri, the once powerful interior minister who embodied Morocco's corruption under Hassan II's reign. New legislation passed to promote the rule of law, and two constitutional referendums expanded the power of parliament and allowed for greater opposition

[29]Ibid.
[30]Maghraoui, "Political Authority in Crisis."
[31]Denoeux and Abdeslam Maghraoui, "King Hassan's Strategy of Political Dualism."
[32]Freedom House, "Egypt," 2.

participation. The king also established a Consultative Council on Human Rights, an organization empowered to investigate current human rights abuses and those of the last three decades, abuses that include thousands of disappearances, torture cases, and arbitrary arrests.[33] Mohammed VI has tried to separate himself from his father's legacy of domination of civil society, creating partnership initiatives between civil organizations that wield significant influence within society.[34]

Under Mohammed VI political dissidents such as Abraham Serfaty and the family of Ben Baraka (a socialist opposition member kidnapped by the Moroccan secret services in Paris in 1965 and never seen again) have been asked to return from exile. And although his party remains illegal, the Islamist leader of the Justice and Benevolent Society, Abdesslam Yassine, was released from house arrest. Further, thousands of political prisoners have been released throughout the 1990s. On the surface, it appears Mohammed VI is breaking from his father's record of human rights abuses by allowing greater democratic practices within the kingdom.

These new developments originated in a set of monarchical liberalization policies under Hassan II in the mid-1980s and early 1990s. In 1992, constitutional amendments gave parliament the authority to reject or approve monarchical government appointments. In 1996, a constitutional amendment allowed all members of the House of Representatives to be elected directly instead of appointed by the monarchy. In 1998, for the first time in Morocco's history, a leader of the opposition movement— Abderrahmane Youssoufi of the USFP (Socialist Union of Popular Forces)—became prime minister. Some argue this was a strategy of cooptation; nevertheless, it brought the opposition a leadership position within the government.[35]

The reforms of the 1990s and into the first decade of the current century have given many democracy enthusiasts reason to celebrate. Some critics, however, remain skeptical, arguing that because the regime continues to manage these developments, democratization remains only apparent and serves to further solidify monarchical control. Others argue that not enough real change has occurred. For example, the new twenty-five-member coalition government established in 2002 continues to closely resemble its predecessor. Nineteen of its members came from the previous

[33]Haddadi, "Two Cheers for Whom? The European Union and Democratization in Morocco"; Scott Macleod, "The King of Cool," Time, 26 June 2000.

[34]Slymovics, "A Truth Commission for Morocco"; Howe, *Morocco.*

[35]Maghraoui, "Democratization in the Arab World," 29–30. Also see Haddadi, "Two Cheers for Whom?" 149–69. The prime minister was later replaced by Driss Jettou, a private entrepreneur in 2002. See also Layachi, "Reform and the Politics of Inclusion in the Maghrib."

cabinet, and its ideological composition was widely criticized as a sign that the palace did not want an effective representative decision-making body.[36] Despite the eased restrictions on public freedoms, the independent media still remain under close scrutiny.[37] The popular anticorruption campaign practically stalled in 2002, and journalists still face repression. Two journalists were detained and interrogated for reporting an interview with an exiled bank president who claimed that the diversion of more than $1 billion from a state bank—uncovered by a judicial investigation—was ordered by unspecified higher-ups in the Moroccan regime. Furthermore, over the summer of 2002, the regime launched a crackdown on radical Islamist groups, continuing a repressive policy against a rather docile Islamic opposition.[38]

Because these new political liberalizing reforms have been part of a dual strategy linked with economic reforms, the regime has had to abide by international stipulations to reform while simultaneously appeasing a populace suffering the crunch of those same economic reforms. Because so much of the current political discourse has focused on the successes and failures of economic reform, some worry that political issues such as the concentration of power in regime hands have been marginalized.[39] Fueling these concerns, the monarchy continues to invent administrative means to limit the power of the supposedly empowered opposition government. Since 1999 Mohammed VI has appointed a political technocratic elite to key positions in the administration and the economy. This elite often has more to say in everyday government affairs than the official opposition movements and cabinet members in government.[40] The most powerful ministerial portfolios—including the Interior Ministry, the strongest of all—remain in the hands of the king's supporters, and the compromised role of the opposition not only improves the king's standing on the international stage but also allows him to deflect some of the blame, in the event that economic and social problems worsen. When things go well, he can take credit for them; but when things turn sour, he can blame the opposition. Ultimately, the king continues to retain veto power over the entire political system.[41] That there has been no sign of

[36]Freedom House, "Egypt," 2.

[37]Maghraoui, "Democratization in the Arab World," 29–30. Also see Haddadi, "Two Cheers for Whom?" 149–69, and Layachi, "Reform and the Politics of Inclusion in the Maghrib."

[38]Maghraoui, "Democratization in the Arab World," 29–30. Also see Haddadi, "Two Cheers for Whom?" 149–69; Layachi, "Reform and the Politics of Inclusion in the Maghrib"; and Lust-Okar, *Structuring Conflict in the Arab World.*

[39]Maghraoui, "Democratization in the Arab World," 24–32.

[40]Ibid., 30.

[41]Najem, "State Power and Democratization in North Africa."

true transfer of power concerns spectators and critics alike. Although the extent of Mohammed VI's true commitment to democratic reform is up for debate, one thing is certain—the legacy of his father continues to define the authoritarian nature of the regime.

Mohammed VI came to power with a desire to bring Morocco into the twenty-first century by improving relations with the European Union and enhancing the country's economic situation. Numerous tasks lay before him. He had inherited an impoverished regime. The country was wracked by a 20% unemployment rate; 8% of the villages were without electricity or running water; and a third of the country lived under the poverty line. With mounting foreign debts (estimated close to $20 billion and approximately 50% of the GDP in 1999) and international pressures to adopt stringent economic reforms, the kingdom today continues to balance its authority by simultaneously tightening and loosening its political grip. It caters to its base of support and is less tolerant to voices of dissent.[42] Such an apparent paradox is possible because governmental power remains completely consolidated within the hands of the monarchy.

HISTORICAL PATTERNS: THE EVOLUTION OF ASSOCIATIONAL LIFE

While the restrictions of Mohammed VI's government polarize the associational terrain along axes of support for and opposition to the regime, associational life in Morocco is vibrant; in the late 1990s, over thirty thousand associations worked in and for all social spheres—health, education, culture, women's rights, orphans, civic education, business, and private enterprise.[43] Around 18% of Moroccans are involved in civic organizations, ranging from women's charitable groups to sports clubs. Although many critics lament their limited autonomy, Morocco's sheer number of associations surely puts it alongside Palestine; both countries have lively civil societies. Morocco's associational terrain has a rich and dynamic history dating to the preindependence era (1956), when a plethora of traditional associations came into existence. These traditional associations normally emerged in specific village and town locales to address the immediate concerns of nearby citizens. These associations included *djama'a, Touiza, Mouzara'a,* and *Mousakat,* categories of informal associations in the rural areas.[44] These charitable self-help organizations dominated the Moroccan associational landscape until the 1980s.

[42]Pripstein, "Globalization and Labor Protection"; United Nations Development Program (UNDP).
[43]Layachi, *State, Society and Democracy in Morocco.*
[44]Ibid.

The Moroccan state realized that the civic sphere was a sector that should not be left for manipulation and penetration by the opposition. To further "clientelize" civil society, it began sponsoring, promoting, and building a pro-regime civic sector. Many newer regional associations such as Ribat al Fath, Fes-Saiss, Bou Regrag, Souss-Casablanca, Angad al Maghreb Acarqui, Hawd Assafi, Doukkal, Ahmed al Hansali, Illigh, AnnahdaNador, and al-Mouhit promote governmental agendas, serve as sites to socialize members into sympathy with regime programs, and function as recruitment venues for pro-regime loyalists.[45] Says Korany, the regime "put at their head its faithful representatives and cronies and supplied them with infrastructure and financial support. The state generosity toward some associations led others to sarcastically label them NGGOs (Nongovernmental governmental NGOS)." Their associational activities were limited to sociocultural activities, sports, arts, and recreations. In the early 1980s, most extant organizations were the creations of persons close to the authorities. Though these associations claimed to be apolitical, they actually were supported by the regime and were used as vehicles for personal ambitions.[46]

Other associations that emerged during this period were, however, overtly political and not pro-regime; they were either linked to political parties or invested in issues that placed pressure on the regime, such as human rights, democracy, and women's rights. The regime was more hesitant to crack down on these new NGOs (although it did), lest it appear too aggressive to an international audience whose donor assistance depended on a record of better human rights and effective democratic reforms.[47] Further, the Moroccan regime realized it could plausibly use these new associations for its own ends. After the economic reforms of the 1980s and 1990s, the Moroccan regime recognized that resources often used to appease the public were in gradual decline. Allowing the emergence of civic associations, the regime rationalized, would allow greater financial demands to be placed on these civic sectors. The regime needed a partner to meet the economic woes of the populace—and what better way to do this than to expand the number of state partners (opposition or not) within the civic sphere?[48]

In response to this growing oppositional civic sector, the regime continued to fund existing associations and allowed new ones to form to bol-

[45] Ibid.; Haddadi, "Two Cheers for Whom?" 149–69.

[46] El-Glaoui, "Contributing to a Culture of Debate in Morocco," 159; Haddadi, "Two Cheers for Whom?" 160.

[47] Haddadi, "Two Cheers for Whom?" 149–169, and Korany, "Restricted Democratization from Above."

[48] El-Glaoui, "Contributing to a Culture of Debate in Morocco," 159; Layachi, *State, Society and Democracy in Morocco;* Korany, "Restricted Democratization from Above."

ster its support in rural areas, co-opting the traditional associations that had characterized Morocco's associational landscape for decades. As the regime continued to scrutinize the activities of political factions and opposition movements, the associational terrain became a safe haven for the mobilization of the opposition. Sa'id Fathallah Oulaalou, leader of the USFP (Socialist Union of Popular Forces) and president of the Moroccan Writer's Union, commented, "Because they were kept out of power, political parties invaded the social field and created associations in order to increase their strength."[49]

Civil society was far from immune to political penetration from both the state and political parties, and its ability to remain unpoliticized and autonomous in ways that "ideal" civil societies are imagined proved difficult.[50] Not only do associations in Morocco not enjoy autonomy, but those associations that wish to remain on the political sidelines are often drawn into the preexisting clash between state and opposition. Sometimes economic necessity dictates succumbing to the pressures of politicization; often, associations succumb to overt regime co-optation and penetration—whether the association members like it or not. At other times, the associations themselves choose their own point on the political axis. Regardless of the sources of the polarizing elements that draw associations to either end of the dichotomy, the ability to remain above or below the fray of politics is virtually impossible.[51]

## ASSOCIATIONS AND THE REGIME

Association leaders often find themselves navigating a close line between regime interests and their own goals and priorities. For example, pro-democracy civil society organizations, especially those concentrated in the women's sector, actively worked for years to obtain a more favorable "women's rights" package—the *mudawana*. This package of personal status rights for women successfully passed into law in 2004. The sheer volume of support for the new law within civil society meant that the king had to either confront a growing and articulate constituency on this issue or incorporate their demands. Soon, the women's organizations realized that there would be more to gain from cooperation with the regime than opposition to it. One leader said, "Before civil society relied largely on international cooperation and the cooperation of embassies here in Morocco. But then the civil society began to work with local elected officials

---

[49] Layachi, *State, Society and Democracy in Morocco.*
[50] Korany, "Restricted Democratization from Above."
[51] Ibid.; Sater, "Civil Society."

to get their work done. Our work with the state, civil society's work with the state, is reflected in the *mudawana* and the preparation of a national program of action."[52]

To move forward on this package of laws, civil society leaders adopted a friendlier stance toward the regime.[53] With the help of the international community, and to win policy changes, these civic associations have had to adopt a more pro-regime line. This neatly illustrates the process of co-optation. Worried that these associations can indeed become the backbone of an autonomous civil society that will eventually weaken the regime, the regime continues, however, to maintain a tight grip on associational activity through a dual strategy of concessions and co-optation. When all else fails, the regime does not hesitate to intervene more aggressively by limiting associations' activities or even exercising further punitive measures. But by using political and economic sanctions and rewards, the regime has successfully curtailed the influence of pro-democracy civic sectors.

The Mohammed V Foundation is a stark example of the regime's clientelistic engineering at work. Headed by Mohammed VI, the foundation funds charitable, development, and infrastructure projects in Moroccan society. These programs aim at keeping would-be oppositional civil society sectors under the firm control of the regime. At the same time, these sectors remain loyal to the regime, because they understand that they are better off with the support of the palace. Said one leader of a microfinance association, "They [the government] listen to us if something doesn't exist that we want, they mobilize things for us. In fact, some of our projects are often funded by money allocated by the government itself."[54] Another association leader is far more pessimistic about the role of government in civil society. She has no connections with the regime and does not desire to enter into any relationship with it. Heading a women's civic association, this leader bluntly states, "We have never worked with elected officials; they don't believe in associations."[55] This sentiment is echoed by another association leader in Rabat who is even fearful of the regime: "Well there was an opening for intellectuals, but there is still repression and there are still arrests."[56]

Many association leaders explained that since Mohammed VI came to power, there has been more purposeful engagement between civil society

---

[52] Alex Kobishyn, supervised by Amaney Jamal, interview with civic associational leader, fall 2005.

[53] Significant pressure was also applied on the regime from international organizations to enhance the status of women in the kingdom.

[54] Alex Kobishyn, supervised by Amaney Jamal, interview with civic association leader, fall 2005.

[55] Ibid.

[56] Ibid.

actors and the regime. Yet what remains less clear is the overall intention the regime has toward these civic sectors. One association leader is extremely skeptical. He, a leader of a civic association dedicated to youth programs, sees regime overtures as a means of co-optation. When asked about the association's relationship with regime officials, he replied by saying: "It is negative. They just want to pretend that there is collaboration with us (on paper). The truth is that when they ask us to a meeting or something, they don't even ask our opinion."[57] The association leaders recognize that, not only does the government not listen to their opinions, but it also tries to promote its popularity and legitimacy when working with them. This same leader was troubled by what he perceived was an apparent government strategy to undermine his association's autonomy. The government offered to help him sponsor a project on youth education but only with "the conditions that we should have to carry their placards and their name. We refused; we wanted to be independent."[58]

While the activities that the regime helps to sponsor seem to be of great importance in Morocco, other observers believe these tactics are aimed at marginalizing the influence of pro-democracy elements of civil society.[59] Through the red tape of administrative political controls, the regime limits the activities of non-regime-supporting associations by denying permits and licenses for associational activities and gatherings.[60] One youth organization even found it difficult to conduct its basic seminars on youth education. "We had a situation in 2001 when the minister of youth forbade us to have activities in youth hostels/homes for whatever reason."[61] The regime, using its systems of "patronage, clientelism, traditionalism, neopatrimonialism," and even intimidation maintains a tight grip on civil society.[62]

## POLITICAL PARTIES AND THE MOROCCAN REGIME

The polarization structuring the associational terrain characterizes larger state-society relations in Morocco. Political parties are at the forefront of the political polarization of pro-regime and anti-regime loyalties that permeate much of the kingdom. The monarchy's most prized resource for controlling political parties has been the lure of political power and

[57]Ibid.

[58]Ibid.

[59]Amaney Jamal, interview with Moroccan professor of sociology, Jan. 2006.

[60]Layachi, *State, Society and Democracy in Morocco.*

[61]Alex Kobishyn, supervised by Amaney Jamal, interview with civic association leader, fall 2005.

[62]Bendourou, "Power and Opposition in Morocco," 116.

legitimacy. Hassan II initially attempted to marginalize and repress political parties, especially opposition parties, but after two military coup attempts, in 1971 and 1972, the king changed his tactics, offering opposition parties that agreed to support the monarchy a place in the government. In part this was a tactic designed to help counter the army.[63] This strategy also caused the leftist UNFP (the National Union of Popular Forces) to splinter from the PI (Istiqlal Party); while the PI joined the government, the USFP (the Socialist Union of Popular Forces), born out of the subdivision within the UNFP in 1974, adopted "a posture of radical dissidence."[64]

Hassan II's stance on political parties established a classic incentive-based system. Parties that support the monarchy were allowed to participate in the government and gained access to valuable resources such as the media. This consequently allowed parties to build a constituency and a base of financial and popular support. Parties that mobilized against the monarchy and its positions were denied the right to exist. According to Bendourou, "thenceforth, parties [had] to subscribe to the official theocratic conception of power, which made the king the temporal and spiritual head of the kingdom." At the same time, opposition movements were not accorded full rights to participate. Hassan II in fact made it very clear that he would have little tolerance for opposition groups. In a 1981 speech, the king sent a daunting message to the opposition: "Hassanian democracy will not be complete, and we will not rest easy, until we teach Moroccans how to practice opposition to the government of the king of Morocco. . . . If we were in opposition, we would say 'we are before anything else servants of the king, who is the king of all Moroccans.'"[65] The opposition had to be extremely careful and acquiescent to regime concerns in order to participate.

Crucially, the USFP illustrates this incentive system at work. The party held firm in its opposition, challenging the regime's leadership until 1982. When the USFP stood in opposition to the king's decision that year to accept a referendum in the Western Sahara, the king jailed the party's leaders and banned its publications and activities.[66] For all practical purposes, the USFP ceased to exist. The PI, as a member of the regime, supported these repressive measures, and eventually the USFP conceded. It agreed to the official line and regained its legal status, albeit at the price of an internal split that gave rise to a new party, al-Talia. Back in the good graces of the monarchy, the USFP allowed one of its leaders to be named to head the Ministry of Cooperation as a show of support for the king's

[63] Ibid., 113.
[64] Ibid., 114.
[65] Ibid., 113.
[66] Ibid.

Western Sahara policy. And in 1998 Youssoufi, the USFP leader jailed in 1982, became prime minister.[67]

Parties that continue to resist the legitimacy of Morocco's regime continue to be excluded from the political process altogether. Several Islamist groups, including Justice and Benevolence, fall into this camp.[68] Up until recent election reforms, the king had other means, besides outright censure and arrest of party members, to control the parties voted into parliament. Maghraoui claims that the regime's most powerful tool has been the election process itself. Since the 1960s, the inclusion of Morocco's political parties was never intended or designed to bring about political change from below. According to Maghraoui, "they were designed to provide a mechanism of elite control and renewal from above through an administrative process of restructuring, reward, exclusion, and co-optation." This way, the monarchy has always been able to select its proponents and opponents alike.[69]

In the 1980s and 1990s, the regime employed several tactics to oversee the electoral process and ensure that the results continued to favor the monarchy. Authorizing the creation of multiple parties—not only to divide the opposition but also to dilute the voices of the populace—was one such method. Others include the gerrymandering of electoral districts to dilute the relatively independent urban vote, the institution of an informal quota system to keep parties on a leash, and, of course, the widespread buying and selling of votes.[70] Thus, if a political party expects to participate in Moroccan government affairs at all, it has to follow the monarchy's unwritten and informal guidelines.

Political parties, potential sites for contestation and competition, instead give credibility to the monarchical system.[71] Nevertheless, the debates between regime and opposition continue to pervade civil society. And as long as opposition movements are denied full access and efficacy within the formal political process, the regime and its opposition will continue to politicize and appropriate civil society for their own agendas.

## THE MEDIA

The Moroccan monarchy continues to regulate freedom of expression tightly, one of the most important resources available to a well-functioning

---

[67]Ibid.
[68]Najem, "State Power and Democratization in North Africa."
[69]Maghraoui, "Political Authority in Crisis," 80.
[70]Ibid.
[71]Lust-Okar, *Structuring Conflict in the Arab World.*

civil and political society. With a population slightly above thirty million, Morocco supports an impressive number of periodical publications—estimated at over five hundred—with over seventeen daily newspapers. Although the print media enjoy some leeway in criticizing the regime, they cannot directly attack the regime. Further, the 2002 Press·Law guarantees that the government has adequate control over the media. Article 29 stipulates that the prime minister may order the suspension of a publication if it misrepresents or undermines Islam, the monarchy, national territorial integrity, or public order.[72] The new law of 2002 makes it easier to obtain a license and start a new publication, and it reduces jail terms for journalists who violate these stipulations, but it still allows for the imprisonment of journalists who undermine the monarchy.

Aside from the financial control that comes from subsidizing the press, the regime also occasionally confiscates copies of publications that cross certain acceptable lines.[73] In 2002, a journalist for the weekly *al-Ayyam* was arrested and briefly detained after he visited Islamist prisoners at the central prison of Kenitra, and two other journalists were given prison sentences, suspended on appeal, for defaming the Moroccan foreign minister. The authorities also seized issues of the French weekly *VSD,* which contained unflattering coverage of the king, and eight thousand copies of the quarterly journal *Wijhat Nadhar,* which contained the transcript of a speech by an opposition leader. In 2003, the Moroccan authorities shut down two newspapers, the French-language *Demain* and the Arabic-language *Douman,* when their editor was jailed for three years for criticizing the regime.[74] Since May 2004, eight Moroccan journalists have been detained with convictions on charges of "insulting the king" and undermining the monarchy, a charge that carries a sentence of eighteen months to three years in prison.[75]

The Moroccan government owns the official press agency, Maghreb Arab Presse, the Radio-Television Marocaine (RTM), the state-run newspaper *Le Matin du Sahara,* and the Arabic daily *al-Anbaa.* These media reflect official government views.[76] Foreign broadcasting and a large independent sector of the media do give Moroccans a variety of news sources, but these sources come under continued pressure from the government.[77]

[72]Bendourou, "Power and Opposition in Morocco," 113–14.
[73]Freedom House, "Morocco," 3–4. 2004.
[74]United Nations Development Program (UNDP).
[75]Fredom House, "Morocco," 2004.
[76]United Nations Development Program (UNDP).
[77]Freedom House, "Morocco," 2004.

## CIVIC ATTITUDES AND ASSOCIATIONAL REALITIES IN MOROCCO

In the case of the state-centralized West Bank, the polarization of civil society into pro- and anti-regime camps resulted in two sectors of the civil society with different measures of civic engagement. The first had close ties to the regime but exhibited lower levels of support for democracy and higher levels of interpersonal trust. The latter exhibited oppositional relations to the regime, and association members in this camp exhibited higher support for democracy and lower levels of interpersonal trust. Morocco substantiates the findings obtained in Palestine—the impact of state-centralized political settings on the differential outcomes of associational life does extend itself to other similarly constructed settings. Association members who are more supportive of the monarchy tend to have higher levels of trust and lower levels of support for democracy. Conversely, association members[78] with lower levels of political confidence in the Moroccan monarchy have lower levels of trust and higher support for democratic institutions.

Throughout the developing world, dominant states amplify the polarization of civil society along pro- and anti-regime axes. This division, bolstered by the strength and dominance of each ruling regime, saturates the associational terrain. The evidence from Morocco and Palestine demonstrates how civic attitudes are directly affected by civil society's relationship to ruling governments. The contextual landscape—in this case, state-centralized political structures—dictates associational life and structures civic engagement. These states will continue to counter-balance the influence of associations within civil society. The results here differ dramatically from those one would expect in states that are not centralized. Here, civic engagement indicators such as interpersonal trust and support for democracy are mediated by regime connections. In the end, interpersonal trust largely appears to support existing state-centralized regimes.

## BEYOND PALESTINE AND MOROCCO: JORDAN AND EGYPT

The associational terrain in Jordan and Egypt is also divided according to political access, clientelism, the availability of funding, and relationships with the regime. As in the Palestinian and Moroccan cases, those sectors of civil society that toe the regime line are accorded preferential status

---

[78]Association members include individuals in community associations, human rights groups, environmental groups, professional associations, youth and sports associations, women's groups, and peace associations.

and enjoy political rights and liberties. Absent data on associational participation in Egypt and Jordan, the remainder of this chapter sketches state-society relations in these two countries, offering a glimpse of political divisions between pro- and anti-regime sectors and how these divisions also penetrate the associational terrain. Bolstering the argument of this book, this section further illustrates the ways in which authoritarian regimes co-opt civic spheres. The inclusion of Egypt (another single-party state) and Jordan (another monarchy) further demonstrates the ways current Arab rulers have marginalized the significance of civil society across various contexts.

The Jordanian monarchy remains authoritarian. In a 2002 document on political conditions in Jordan, Freedom House reported:

> The King has long been the center of political authority in this country. . . . While organized political activity is actively encouraged in Jordan, the Government continues to use its institutional powers, as well as sporadic instances of fraud and intimidation to weaken opposition to the King and his policies.[79]

The regime banned political parties until 1989, when the first elections since 1966 were held. Although the events of the 1990s led many scholars to assume that Jordan was slowly heading toward more political liberalization, since the beginning of his reign in 1999 King Abdullah has adopted a slate of emergency laws that have effectively reversed much of the democratic advancement. In 2002, the government limited freedom of speech, expression, and assembly.[80]

The Jordanian monarchy continues to monitor all facets of political society. It allows associations to form, but they cannot be political. When, in the eyes of the regime, civic associations threaten the political status quo, the monarchy does not hesitate to step in by intimidating, harassing, or even imprisoning members, and closing down associations. These tactics of intimidation extend to other sectors of civil society. The Mukhabarat (state security apparatus), for instance, must approve all journalists operating in the kingdom. The government continues to own the country's news agency and radio and television stations.[81] Despite some efforts to curb censorship, the king amended the Press and Publications Law, restricting the opposition party press (the main conduit of party information) and increasing penalties for printing materials deemed objectionable.[82] The opposition has also alleged that the regime

[79]Freedom House, "Egypt," 2002.
[80]Ryan and Schwedler, "The Return to Elections"; Lucas, "Deliberalization in Jordan."
[81]Cunningham, "Jordan's Information Revolution," 5.
[82]Lust-Okar, "The Decline of Jordanian Political Parties," 561.

attempts to co-opt parliamentarians with tempting offers of ministerial appointments and lucrative business contracts. As Quintan Wictorow-itcz concludes, "State power does not necessarily entail raw, coercive force or repression. Through the selective application and manipulation of bureaucratic rules, procedures, and processes, regimes can effectively project state power through less visible mechanisms of social control."[83] In this regard, the Jordanian monarchy is very much embedded within civil society.

King Hussein dissolved the Jordanian parliament before the 1993 elections because he was unhappy with increased opposition; he later implemented the Electoral Election Law of 1993, significantly decreasing the size of the opposition in parliament. The 1992 Political Parties Law made it illegal for parties to have external ties and funding. For secular parties with connections to external organizations—in Iraq, Syria, Palestine, and the former Soviet Union—these laws were challenging.[84] Thus, the monarchy has made the success of any resource-poor parties dependent on the regime. In response, opposition parties in the 1990s formed broad coalitions using national conferences to coordinate their positions and bolster support.[85] Yet their relative influence remains checked by the regime, and political authority remains firmly fixed in the regime and in regime-authorized channels.

Officially, Egypt has a presidential political system. The constitution of 1971 established a six-year presidency and an elected parliament. Practically, though, Egypt often resembles a semibenevolent totalitarian regime. A 2003 Freedom House report described the Egyptian political system thus: "There is no competitive process for the election of the Egyptian president; the public is entitled only to confirm in a national referendum the candidate nominated by the People's Assembly [the lower house of parliament] for a six year term."[86] The 454-seat assembly "has limited influence on government policy, and almost all legislation is initiated by the executive."[87] President Mubarak's National Democratic Party (NDP) dominates the assembly. Established and financed by the government, the NDP is empowered to provide social services and deliver on promises thus enhancing its standing.[88] The upper house, the Consultative Council (Majlis al-Shura), is two-thirds elected, but it functions only in an advisory capacity.[89] The NDP dominates both houses and—by means of election

[83] Wictorowitcz, "State Power," 695. See also Brand, "Displacement for Development?"
[84] Lust-Okar, "The Decline of Jordanian Political Parties," 558.
[85] Ibid., 561.
[86] Freedom House, "Egypt," 2003.
[87] Ibid.
[88] Korany, "Restricted Democratization from Above."
[89] Ibid., 62–63.

irregularities and government control over political resources—regularly finds itself reelected and returned to power.

Much of the Mubarak government's power comes from the "state of emergency" that has existed since 1967. President Anwar al-Sadat suspended emergency rule for five months in 1981, but following Sadat's assassination, Mubarak reinstated emergency provisions.[90] Subsequently, the government rationalized the continuation of emergency rule as a necessary tool in the fight against Islamist radicals.[91] While Islamic groups such as Al-Jihad, Al-Jama'a Al-Islamiyya, and the less violent Muslim Brotherhood face the most severe persecution, the emergency laws also target and regulate other social and political groups. These laws enable the regime to establish special security courts that function outside the jurisdiction of existing laws to protect citizens. Emergency law (Law no. 162, of 1958, as amended) also allows the regime to censor, confiscate, and close newspapers on the grounds of "public safety" and "national security" and to detain without trial or charge anyone suspected of being a threat to national security and public order.[92]

The regime continues to produce and enforce legislation that does not differ significantly from laws ruled unconstitutional by the court, effectively sidestepping unfavorable judicial decisions. This includes the new Association Law approved by the People's Assembly in 2002, purportedly an amended version of legislation rejected by the Constitutional Court in 2000. The law, however, contains many of the same vaguely worded restrictions on associational life that appeared in the 2000 version.[93]

The Egyptian regime can manipulate the political and social atmosphere in Egypt at will. Political parties, nongovernmental associations, and all public demonstrations, rallies, and protests must acquire licensing from government organizations or ministries, licenses that are often arbitrarily refused. Political dissent is stifled because the government owns and operates all broadcast media. Although a number of private newspapers exist, the regime indirectly controls them through its monopoly on printing and distribution. Vague statues in the Press Law, the Publications Law, the penal code, and libel laws significantly hamper press freedom. As in Morocco, criticism of the Egyptian president and his family can result in the imprisonment of journalists and the closure of publications.[94] Definitions of acceptable language and discourse are vague, yet those parties and organizations that fail to conform to these expectations risk censorship, confiscation of their publications, arrest, and intimidation of their

[90]Brownlee, "The Decline of Pluralism," 5–6.
[91]Singerman, "The Politics of Emergency Rule in Egypt," 30.
[92]Ibid., 29–30.
[93]Ibid., 4.
[94]Ibid.

members—even disbandment. These conditions have promoted the polarization of Egypt's political and civil life around either the NDP and the president or the opposition movements. Social and political organizations that choose to use government resources must practice self-censorship.

## ASSOCIATIONAL LIFE IN JORDAN AND EGYPT

The Jordanian and Egyptian regimes are blatantly authoritarian. Their ability to micromanage their civic spheres—albeit in differing ways—results in a system of rewards and sanctions founded on support for the government. Although these countries have seen a growth in civic associations in the last two decades, these associations find themselves in one of two camps. They either become (or are created for the sole purpose of being) supportive of the palace, or they find their associations disadvantaged and marginalized in their civic spheres. Political contestation, emanating from the wellsprings of associational life, is suppressed.

Modern Egypt has a surprising number of vital voluntary associations, NGOs, charities, parties, and syndicates, especially considering their close regulation by the authorities.[95] This number is indeed remarkable, given the regime's use of wide-ranging, catchall decrees that allow it to intervene in the management or the financial dimensions of these organizations as well as to prohibit or even merge associations at will. In 1996, more than 25,000 civil society organizations (CSOs) existed in Egypt, including "15,000 CSOs registered under the 1964 law; 5,000 cooperative organizations; 4,000 youth and sporting clubs; 30 professional associations; and 14 political parties."[96] The tenacity of Egyptian civil life is perhaps due to the long-standing prominence of social associations in Egypt's political system. For decades, while Britain ruled the country, these associations played key service and welfare roles. Under Nasser's and Sadat's reigns, however, tighter governmental restrictions stifled the efficacy of civic associations.

During the 1980s and 1990s civil society organizations enjoyed greater freedoms in Egypt and in many other Middle Eastern countries.[97] The Egyptian government licensed hundreds of new publications and allowed professional syndicates a higher level of involvement in shaping political life, as the number of political parties increased and NGOs expanded.[98] This was especially true of business and professional groups, which were

---

[95] Zubaida, "Islam in Contemporary Egypt," 246.
[96] Ibrahim, "Reform and Frustration in Egypt," 131.
[97] Rahman, "The Politics of 'Uncivil' Society in Egypt," 25.
[98] Ibid.

able to influence the direction of economic reform. After a period of political liberalization, however, the regime has increasingly limited opportunities for the dispersal of power beyond the president.[99]

Different associational strains—Islamic, Coptic, advocacy, and research NGOs—have dominated the space newly opened for social and political activity. Islamic and Coptic organizations often work through social aid organizations intended to provide basic services such as health care and education to their respective communities. Advocacy groups, such as human rights and election watch organizations, are usually more explicitly political and more likely to directly criticize the regime.[100] Autonomous research organizations and think tanks, such as the Ibn Khaldoun Center founded in 1988, have also played a key role in the expansion of Egyptian civil society.[101]

In Jordan, despite an extensive program of political liberation that allowed parliamentary elections and the operation of political parties, the monarchy's implementation of a system of administrative and bureaucratic carrots polarizes the civic space within the kingdom. The monarchy requires all social development societies to be members of the General Union of Voluntary Societies (GUVS—*al-ittihad al-'amm lil-jama'iyyat al-khairyiyya*), an umbrella organization administered by the state, the chief purpose of which is to monitor and bind associational activity to the regime. Once a member organization obtains its operating permit from the GUVS, the monarchy bestows a small stipend on it and restricts it from receiving outside funding. Thus, the member associations find themselves under the control of the government. The regime's heavy-handed involvement in civic affairs restricts their organizational programs and activities.[102]

Social groups are by law prohibited from political activity; in practice, however, the monarchy allows them to exist if they support the government. Aside from according them legitimacy (and the right to exist), the monarchy's approval also grants them access to financial resources and the mostly government-controlled media. The government closely monitors these supposedly neutral associations for any missteps, no matter how minor.

Since the outlawing of political parties in 1956, various professional groups and unions have arisen to fill the void. Union membership includes doctors, engineers, lawyers, dentists, pharmacists, journalists, writers, geologists, and agricultural engineers.[103] Despite strict laws regulating

[99]Brownlee, "The Decline of Pluralism," 6.
[100]Rahman, "The Politics of 'Uncivil' Society in Egypt," 30.
[101]Khalifa, "Reviving Civil Society in Egypt," 156.
[102]Lowrance, "After Beijing," 4.
[103]Brand, "'In the Beginning,'" 166.

what activities a social association might participate in, these professional unions were able to become important political entities. During martial law, they continued to hold democratic elections and occasionally attempted to put together broader, nongovernmental councils to address the pressing political issues of the day.[104] These moments of social advocacy, however, often proved fatal. The government disbanded the Professional Grouping association, a group formed of labor and professional union representatives in response to the 1967 Israeli defeat of its Arab neighbors and seizure of the West Bank, *despite* the association's attempts to stay in constant contact with the government regarding political issues. Although the king attended the first meeting of the group's founding organization, the National Grouping (al-Tajammu' al-Watani), he eventually disbanded it when its activity became too intrusive.[105] As long as the organization conveniently mobilized public opinion favorable to the monarchy, the regime permitted it a degree of political activity. The union continued to function after 1971, but it could not engage in any coordinated professional or trade union activity.[106]

## CIVIL SOCIETY AND POLARIZATION

Historically, the Jordanian regime prevented the operation of civic associations if they possessed overt political objectives. Under the Voluntary Associations Law no. 33, the Jordanian regime has the right to enter the offices of any NGO to review its records. As Sherri Lowrance has pointed out, this law "prohibit[ed] any NGO from trying to achieve 'political goals.'" The law was historically used against NGOs that opposed regime policy.[107] The government, more recently, has preferred to devise complicated administrative restrictions on civil society instead of resorting to violence and physical intimidation.[108] Censorship of organizations' publications, withdrawal of access to other types of media, reorganization of the NGOs' governing bodies, and the writing of association constitutions are all common practice for the regime. Of course other techniques, including arresting members or leaders, blacklisting, and the closing of the organization, are also feasible options exercised on the most unruly associations.

Labor unions and women's organizations have faced similar challenges from the 1960s onward. Both types of organizations were theoretically

[104] Ibid., 167.
[105] Ibid., 166.
[106] Ibid.
[107] Lowrance, "After Beijing," 3.
[108] "Political Rights and Censorship in Jordan," 34.

allowed to exist, provided they did not participate in political activity; however, because of the Federation of Trade Unions' (FTUJ) 1970 involvement in the Jordanian civil war, the government has pursued a course of action that severely undermined the organization. The FTUJ called for reconciliation with the Palestinian resistance and staged repeated demonstrations in hopes of winning fair wage compensation and safer working conditions. These activities, rightly understood as political, could have wreaked havoc with the Jordanian status quo. In response, the government first dissolved the acting executive committee of the FTUJ, replacing it with members who were more sympathetic to the regime. The Jordanian monarchy swiftly amended the organization's constitution to allow for greater government access to union activities. When these new tactics did not accomplish their goal, the government adopted more direct means. The regime convinced potential candidates not to run and imprisoned activists or dismissed them from their jobs. By the mid-1980s the government had gained control of most unions and intimidated most citizens.[109]

Women's social associations faced similar obstacles. In the early 1980s leaders of these associations had their passports confiscated and were consequently unable to gain employment. The Interior Ministry closed the Women's Union in Jordan (WUJ) (*jam'iyyat al-nisa' al-'arabiyyat fi al-urdun*) in response to its support of Palestinian rights. Although the high court ruled in favor of the union, the WUJ did not have the resources to implement the decision once the union was dissolved. Subsequent to the union's demise, the government formed the General Federation of Jordanian Women (GFJW) to replace the WUJ.[110] Unlike the WUJ, the GFJW—a puppet association for the regime—had no real program.

The government has also encouraged the development of charitable societies to address issues surrounding poverty, children, disability, health, and the elderly.[111] These types of associations, considered suitable for women, are not politically threatening. While the government has considered this gendered form of civic participation safe, it resisted when women began to make demands on issues of equal rights, accountability for honor killings, and full economic integration.[112]

This constant government intervention into the associations' activities inevitably polarized civic life. Groups that wished to survive and receive invaluable government resources chose to support the monarchy. Small social associations opposed to the regime's actions on any one issue were easily influenced or disbanded. As a result, opposition groups were forced

[109]Ibid., 169.
[110]Lowrance, "After Beijing," 6.
[111]Janine Clark, *Islam, Charity and Activism.*
[112]Brand, *Civil Society in the Middle East,* 176.

to unite to gain any significant amount of sway over the regime. For organizations such as the National Grouping and the General Secretariat of Patriotic and Popular Forces in Jordan (formed after the 1982 Israeli invasion of Lebanon), the combination of political views under one umbrella organization often caused irresolvable conflicts between members that spelled an early death for the nascent association.[113]

In Egypt, nonprofit charitable associations and private voluntary organizations (PVOs) come under the stifling authority of the Ministry of Social Affairs. A law enacted after the 1952 revolution to control associational life established state supervision over associations, foundations, and professional groups. These are given access to the "massive resources" of the state but must, in exchange, face the bureaucratic impediments under which state-sponsored institutions operate.[114] The government does not so strongly interfere with nonprofit limited-liability firms created under the Companies Law of Egypt, but these NGOs must deal with severe budgetary constraints. In addition, nongovernmental periodicals face restrictions. A license is needed, and with it comes the scrutiny and tediousness of numerous official oversights.[115]

Individuals and organizations that try not to express explicit allegiance with either side are often labeled regardless of any preference for neutrality. The regime sees most criticism as de facto opposition and treats it accordingly. The arrest of Saad Eddin Ibrahim, the chairman of the Ibn Khaldoun Center for Development Studies, and his two assistants in June of 2000 provides a telling example. Shortly after the arrests, the government shut down the center itself. The allegations against Ibrahim centered on the claim that he had accepted foreign funds without government permission. In actuality, it is widely believed that the regime's actions against the Ibn Khaldoun Center were designed as a broader warning to Egyptian civil society groups to refrain from their demands for human rights and democracy.[116] In a statement to the state security prosecutors, Ibrahim emphasized that his arrest came in response to the center's research on issues such as election fraud, women's rights, and the mistreatment of the Copts, a Christian minority.[117] The center served predominantly as a research center whose main purpose was to educate, raise social awareness, and promote serious discussion of various social issues.

The Egyptian state has taken steps to sequester professional syndicates that were once "considered . . . secular, Westernized, and supportive of

[113] Ibid., 166–67.

[114] Khalifa, "Reviving Civil Society in Egypt," 156.

[115] Ibid., 160.

[116] Ibrahim, "A Reply to My Accusers," 58–59; for details of the arrest see Singerman, "The Politics of Emergency Rule in Egypt," 31.

[117] Ibrahim, "A Reply to My Accusers," 58–59.

the government" but have become dominated, through internal election processes, by members of the Muslim Brotherhood.[118] In an attempt to deprive the Brotherhood of twenty of its most dynamic young candidates in the 2000 parliamentary elections, security forces arrested them.[119] The group, which comprised mostly lawyers, university professors, and other professionals, was accused of membership in an illegal organization and dictating the activities of professional organizations.[120] In this way, the regime not only uses its resources to control the Brotherhood when it finds it convenient to do so but also hides behind the issue of Islamic radicalism while it limits other types of associational life.[121]

In 2002 the People's Assembly passed a new law regulating civic associations. The new law, replacing law 32 of 1964, bans political activity and the receipt of foreign funding without government approval, grants the Ministry of Social Affairs the power to dissolve NGOs, and eliminates legal loopholes that allowed human rights groups to avoid NGO restrictions by registering as law firms or civic groups.[122] In addition, the law heavily restricts the formation and activities of labor unions and prohibits strikes, making the government-backed Egyptian Trade Union Federation the only legal labor federation.[123]

While it is clearly true that intimidation is a viable tool, the Egyptian government has other means readily available. Says Singerman,

> As Egypt's activists—whether promoting human rights, women's rights, minority rights, sexual freedom, democratization, or Islamist ideas— pursue their goals and aims, they are constantly confronted by a morass of legal bureaucratic ambiguity. In particular, the multilayered government regulation that emanates from ever-growing and mutating bureaucratic bodies keeps those who are pushing the political envelope unstable and insecure. The legal and bureaucratic ambiguity of the Egyptian state, many lawyers believe, is intentional, since it allows the regime flexibility and multiple strategies to pursue its critics, whether they are NGOs, civil companies, media publications, or individual activists.[124]

This maze of legal regulations surrounds Egypt's civil society, allowing the state's direct and self-interested interference and stifling the "civil society" project more broadly.

---

[118]Singerman, "The Politics of Emergency Rule in Egypt," 31.
[119]Sivan, "Arabs and Democracy," 78.
[120]Singerman, "The Politics of Emergency Rule in Egypt," 31.
[121]Janine Clark, *Islam, Charity and Activism.*
[122]Freedom House, "Egypt," 4.
[123]Ibid., 5.
[124]Singerman, "The Politics of Emergency Rule in Egypt," 32.

The Egyptian regime continues to create new laws to regulate the civic sector. The 1993 Unified Law for Syndicates, for instance, allowed the government greater authority to intervene directly in the internal elections of professional syndicates.[125] The government used this law to decrease the influence of Islamists who had gained power as board members of important syndicates including the physicians', the engineers', and the pharmacists' professional associations. The use of the obscure Military Decree no. 4 of 1992 to charge Professor Saad Eddin Ibrahim with illegally accepting funds from the European Commission for a voter registration project has served to prevent other NGOs from relying on foreign funding.[126] The law, requiring all NGOs to obtain government approval of both their establishment and their activities, as well as approval for the receipt of foreign funds, was used to deny the Egyptian Organization for Human Rights—the oldest human rights group in the country—a license to operate officially. In 1998, after thirteen years of operation, the organization was forced to decline further Western funding and scale back its activities in response to the arrest of the organization's secretary-general, Hafez Abu Saeda.[127] Reliance on domestic sources for funding has strengthened the clientelistic relationship between civil society and the current governing regime. Already, major intellectuals, literary figures, and journalists are primarily employed by the state in public universities, government publishing houses, and theaters. They are also affiliated with state-sponsored think tanks and dependent on the state in a variety of ways.[128]

In Egypt and Jordan, the impact associational life can have on democratization is constrained by the overall political context. The state permeates every sector of civil society and undermines the ability of other actors to influence change. Civil society sectors are often co-opted; if they resist co-optation, they face serious repercussions. Viable civil societies—civil societies that have the ability to expand and extend their networks—are closely linked to the state. In short, the state dominates civil society.

## CONCLUSION

Developments across the Middle East, especially with the international community's demands for greater democratization, leave some room for optimism. Nevertheless, the security situation in most of these countries is also a pressing concern. In May 2004, Morocco suffered a series of

---

[125]Rahman, "The Politics of 'Uncivil' Society in Egypt," 29.
[126]Singerman, "The Politics of Emergency Rule in Egypt," 31.
[127]Brownlee, "The Decline of Pluralism," 8.
[128]Singerman, "The Politics of Emergency Rule in Egypt," 34.

suicide bombings. In October 2005, Jordan witnessed a series of bombings. Egypt has experienced new forms of opposition and protest, and remains worried about future incidents of violence. Thus, while the regimes have progressed with promises of democratization, they are in fact simultaneously moving their civil and political liberties backward. Security concerns remain paramount, which translates literally into reduced liberties at all levels. The recent deterioration in press freedoms in Morocco, for instance, appears to be a result of the government crackdown following the May 2004 bombings. The regime has used an antiterrorism law, which it passed soon after the attacks, to repeatedly detain reporters.[129]

With reduced liberties comes less autonomy for associations and civil society. If civil societies remain the first casualty of increased security measures, then the future of civil society in the Arab world remains bleak—especially if we consider that democracy promotion in the region has been accompanied by American involvement in Iraq, fueling terrorist sensibilities all the more. Security and political stability rather than democracy will be a major focus of the next several years. For democrats across the Arab world, this will surely mean a much more arduous journey as they continue to work for democratic freedoms and openings. The challenges they face are staggering. Not only are regimes firmly in control chipping away at their existing freedoms (however few those already are), but stability and security concerns grant regimes greater incentives to continue monopolization and centralization of power. With international spectators and observers concerned about the Islamist threat, regimes have far more leeway in implementing stricter authoritarian practices.

[129]Freedom House, "Egypt," 2004.

# CHAPTER SIX

# Conclusion: Toward a Theory of Democratic Citizenship in State-Centralized Nations

> Good government creates a good citizen. You cannot have
> a good citizen without a good government. [Good govern-
> ment includes] basic law, constitution, free and fair elections,
> separation of powers, accountability. . . . I am not inventing
> anything new.
> —Palestinian associational leader, 1999[1]

CIVIC ENGAGEMENT, support for democratic institutions, and interpersonal trust appear to be essential components of making democracy work. Theory and observation often lead us to think that social trust enhances the performance of political institutions and states. Cooperation cannot function without trust. Without cooperation, civic interactions, and reciprocal norms of behavior, community becomes meaningless—an empty category.[2] A lively community is one that cares about local matters and issues, and is engaged with current developments. In turn, where people hold officials accountable and share information, better government performance tends to encourage people to trust those they do not know. Well-functioning institutions that treat people equally create disincentives to behavior that violates trust, offer models of cooperation, and lessen resentments. Thus, the relationship between trust and civic engagement is endogenous and reciprocal.

## INTERPERSONAL TRUST AND ASSOCIATIONAL REALITIES IN THE WEST BANK

> We do all our work for the state, to help them with their
> capacity and institution building. There is no point in working
> in a vacuum. One has to work with the state. Otherwise we
> will have "lost" input.
> —pro-PNA associational leader, 1999[3]

---

[1] Amaney Jamal, interview with anti-PNA associational leader CLP, summer 1999.

[2] Putnam, *Making Democracy Work;* Coleman, *The Foundations of Social Theory;* Ulsaner, *Social Capital and Participation in Everyday Life.*

[3] Amaney Jamal, interview with JAD, summer 1999.

Interpersonal trust has been linked to greater life satisfaction and more effective democracy.[4] Some, such as Samuel Huntington, however, link interpersonal trust to political trust, a correlation that accords legitimacy to governing institutions, and view this formula as an important element for political stability.[5] For scholars such as Robert Putnam, social trust increases political trust; for Levi and Huntington, political trust produces social trust.[6] Still others link trust to social cooperation benefiting civic engagement, which is in turn important for democracy.[7] After all, the notion that citizens actively participate in government rests at the core of democratic citizenship. Taking a slightly different approach, Eric Uslaner argues that individuals with higher levels of trust are more likely to be involved in societal projects such as charitable and voluntary associations, and he further finds that individuals with higher levels of trust are more likely to make charitable donations and help others.[8] He also argues that polities characterized by greater economic asymmetry among social classes have decreased levels of interpersonal trust, and he contends that the inducements to generalized levels of interpersonal trust are context-driven.

Most studies that examine corruption and clientelism point out that levels of interpersonal trust are lower among the citizens of polities characterized by high levels of corruption. As Francis Fukuyama writes of China and Latin America, "Families are strong and cohesive, but it is hard to trust strangers, and levels of honesty and cooperation in public life are much lower. A consequence is nepotism and pervasive public corruption."[9] Although my study demonstrates similar findings, three vital, qualitative distinctions differentiate my work from that of other scholars.[10] First, lower levels of interpersonal trust were in fact found among those association members who were strong supporters of democratic institutions. The relationship between levels of interpersonal trust and levels of support for democratic institutions was a directly inverse one. Further, supporters of democratic institutions were more likely than nonsupporters

---

[4]Almond and Verba, *The Civic Culture;* Muller and Seligson, "Civic Culture and Democracy"; Inglehart, *Culture Shift.*

[5]Huntington, *Political Order in Changing Societies.*

[6]Putnam, *Making Democracy Work* and *Bowling Alone;* Levi, "Making Democracy Work"; Huntington, *Political Order in Changing Societies.*

[7]Putnam, *Making Democracy Work* and *Bowling Alone.*

[8]Ulsaner, "Democracy and Social Capital" and *Social Capital and Participation in Everyday Life.*

[9]Fukuyama, "Social Capital," 99.

[10]Average levels of social trust in the West Bank are lower than in other parts of the world. I argue that once you average the levels of trust after combining those of pro-PNA supporters with those of non-PNA supporters, the sum is lower than in other countries that do not have to average stark opposing norms.

to score higher on civic engagement indicators. Second, members of pro-regime associations were more trustful, but their levels of support for democratic institutions were lower. Those association members with lower levels of support for democratic institutions also exhibited lower levels of civic engagement. Although they possessed higher levels of trust because of their involvement in the clientelistic networks of the PNA, they had become embedded within its overall structure. Third, these pro-PNA association members attained their individual interests through their clientelistic ties to the government, precluding any necessity to cooperate with others.

Based on these findings, social trust has no apparent link to patterns of democratic citizenship. A dramatic rise in interpersonal trust among West Bank Palestinians, if accompanied by no tangible reforms in the ranks of the PNA, would raise serious doubts about the prospects for democratization through associational membership. These findings are consistent with current work on the subject that argues not all forms of trust are benevolent. Joji Watanuki, for instance, argues that embeddedness in dense social relationships and membership in traditional nonvoluntary associations generate social capital that is bad for democracy.[11] Nancy Rosenblum, Mark Warren, Robert Putnam, and others argue that associational type—based on its vision or composition—may produce forms of social capital that are not necessarily good for civic engagement and democratic governance.[12] Most of these studies argue that the "type" of association or its political program explains the valence of social trust generated, limiting their analysis to internal associational characteristics that mediate the type of trust formed. I argue that, as in the case of the West Bank, these internal associational qualities are indeed important, but the political context is even more important. In an environment such as the West Bank, where associational life is structured along vigorous pro- and anti-PNA dimensions, associations that were clients of the state reproduced vertical ties between their members and the state. Once absorbed into the whims of the governing power, those associations most benevolent in form and purpose became hierarchically structured, clientelistic sites. Pro-PNA association members joined to obtain services and fulfill needs, to "help out," in some form. Many saw their involvement as aiding the Palestinian national project. And many more, after enjoying the ease of clientelistic access, saw very little wrong with their forms of civic participation.

Association members with higher levels of interpersonal and social

[11] Watanuki, quoted in Pharr, "Officials Misconduct and Public Distrust: Japan and the Trilateral Democracies," 187.

[12] Rosenblum, *Membership and Morals;* Warren, *Democracy and Association.*

trust also had higher levels of political confidence in the regime. In a sense, the literature that underscores the importance of interpersonal trust for political trust is compatible with my findings here.[13] But while most studies link interpersonal trust to support of democratic governing institutions, my study demonstrates that trust also significantly describes support of authoritarian rule. Although the paths that lead to these levels of interpersonal trust in the West Bank and those based on (or envisioned within) democratic frameworks are in fact different, the outcome—more interpersonal trust—appears to be directly linked to confidence in the government. Examining the sources of interpersonal trust, the mechanisms that produce it, and the sources that sustain it is imperative in any examination of the impact of interpersonal trust on civic engagement and democratic governance.

Two factors broadly structure levels of interpersonal trust. The first inducement of generalized trust is straightforward. Does the state look out for the interests of its citizens, does the rule of law apply to all, and does the state have the resources and legitimacy to uphold the law uniformly in society? These factors determine whether average citizens can trust strangers or even desire to communicate with them. A citizen may understand the importance of a cooperative relationship, but the potential costs of cooperation may outweigh the benefits. Governments must supply the context in which cooperation can operate. Levels of trustworthiness also structure trust. Where expectations of a trusting relationship are met, there are incentives to continue to trust or to expand on those relationships.[14]

Governments and citizens together create the necessary foundations of social trust. Where citizens see little incentive to cooperate, there is little incentive to trust. Democratic governance creates incentives for citizens to collectivize in purposeful ways to influence policy—because channels of influence and participation are open to all citizens equally. Nondemocracies create many incentives—for citizens with ready access to the government. It is no surprise that among association members in the good graces of the PNA, levels of interpersonal trust were higher. Accorded government protections, their criteria of trustworthiness were low because they did not need the cooperation of other citizens to achieve their ends. Therefore, they had fewer reasons to engage others in

---

[13]For a comprehensive overview of this position, see Pharr and Putnam, *Disaffected Democracies.*

[14]Hardin, *Trust and Trustworthiness;* Robert Wuthnow says: "People understand trust in conditional terms, meaning that they implicitly or explicitly assume that it is reasonable or possible to trust *if certain conditions are met.* How they frame their talk about trust is usually an indication of what these conditions are." Wuthnow, "The Role of Trust in Civic Renewal," 215.

order to achieve their interests. Clearly, associational life can give credibility and legitimacy to a nondemocratic government.

The type of trust prevalent among pro-PNA association members is not necessarily good for democratic outcomes. But from the perspective of the PNA and its supporters, this form of trust has been good because it has generated support and legitimacy for the PNA. Social science research would clearly benefit from an understanding of the mechanisms and processes that produce trust; such understanding would allow social science research to better comprehend the role of trust in a given society. As interpersonal trust can have a neutral valence, so, too, can interpersonal distrust—only when one places trust in its appropriate context can one fully understand what structures it and its correlated effects.

## CIVIC ENGAGEMENT, SUPPORT FOR DEMOCRATIC INSTITUTIONS, AND ASSOCIATIONAL REALITIES IN THE WEST BANK

> The most important thing is the expression of opinion. In many cases, they pretend there is freedom of expression, but when we express that there is a problem with the PNA, we may get in trouble. We do not have the opportunity to criticize our leaders with freedom and the media. All our Arab countries claim they are democratic, but they are wrong.
> —Palestinian anti-PNA associational leader, 1999[15]

Levels of civic engagement and support for democratic institutions were higher among anti-PNA association members than among pro-PNA association members. Levels of interpersonal trust, however, were lower among anti-PNA association members. This does not correspond with current understandings, which often consider levels of civic engagement and interpersonal trust as mutually reinforcing. But the underpinnings of this difference become clearer once we take into account the polarized political setting of the West Bank. Association members who were not clients of the PNA were more likely to engage other members to satisfy community needs, to discuss and address local politics, and to obtain up-to-date community news. Because their organizations were not vertically linked to the government, they were also more likely to depend on one another to achieve common goals. These anti-PNA associations were thus structured horizontally.

[15]Amaney Jamal, interview with TAH, summer 1999.

Through these horizontal networks, democrats sustained their interest in their communities. In these associations, they discussed matters relating to current political trends and assessed the influence of overall social developments on their lives. The associations also served as sites where individuals engaged with and learned from one another, and as forums that reinforced and enhanced levels of civic competence among anti-PNA association members. Karol Edward Soltan argues that civic competence is composed of the "mental qualities required for successful participation in government." He further says, "We now see that strengthening civic competence in the population continues the battle that was fought for the extension of citizen rights."[16] Yet increases in civic competence without the necessary structural and institutional changes to absorb increased citizen awareness can also lead to the marginalization of civil society.

In anti-PNA associations, higher levels of civic engagement and support for democratic institutions indicated higher levels of civic competence. Since anti-PNA association members had low opinions of the PNA, they were more likely to discuss the abuses of the ruling government among themselves. Often, these members talked about the freedoms and rights afforded citizens in democratic countries while lamenting their lot in an authoritarian setting and discussing the abuses of the PNA. Taking great pride in their nationality and having great faith in their potential human capital, Palestinian citizens awaited the day when they would be allowed to freely reveal their true capabilities.

Associations can increase the civic competence of members; thus, they can potentially become schools for democratic education. Yet, democratic education—an increased appreciation for the rights and duties associated with citizenship—need not correlate with other important indictors also deemed useful for successful democracy, such as interpersonal trust. Among association members, civic engagement, civic competence, and support for democratic institutions also highly correlated with dissatisfaction with government and higher faith in the overall concept of citizenship. As Soltan continues, "A citizen is someone who cares about how well the political institutions work in his or her own society. Such a citizen wants to make these institutions the best they can be—and the specific competences of an ideal citizen follow from this commitment."[17]

One of the components of civic engagement in this analysis is political, knowledge.[18] In *The Third Wave,* Samuel Huntington elaborates a "domino effect": citizens across the world are beginning to see them-

[16]Soltan, "Introduction," 2–3.
[17]Ibid.
[18]Democrats in my sample, as illustrated in chapter 4, scored higher on questions gauging their levels of participation in political events and activities in Palestinian society.

selves as part of a larger global, democratic community, and share similar values about civic rights.[19] Globalization, rather than civic ties to their own governing polities, nurtures these democratic attitudes for many in the developing world. These democrats have little faith in their ruling regimes; their allegiance instead rests with a common ideal. To what commonwealth do the actively engaged citizenries of the nondemocratic world belong? They obviously belong not to "their" governments.

## CIVIC ENGAGEMENT AND INTERPERSONAL TRUST AMONG ASSOCIATION MEMBERS

In the West Bank, pro-PNA association members could be more trusting of others because of their pro-government ties; their trust in others derived from the mediator and guarantor of that trust. Because they had confidence in a higher authority, pro-PNA association members possessed the luxury to see others as trustworthy. Clientelistic ties guaranteed that their trust would not be exploited. The compatibility of interpersonal trust and political trust was apparent among pro-PNA association members in the West Bank, but there existed no significant relationship between interpersonal trust and levels of civic engagement. In the West Bank, social trust did not correlate to civic engagement among association members; rather, it was more closely linked to confidence in public institutions. These findings pose an interesting puzzle. If those members who were more engaged did not possess the trust necessary to seek out one another in collective communal endeavors, did their civic engagement remain unused? If we are concerned only about outcomes, the answer is yes; however, I am interested in understanding the mechanisms and pathways that produced these outcomes.

Only when analyzing the political context of the West Bank did these outcomes make sense. In democracies, the democratic institutions of the state make necessary the incentives for cooperative and collective behavior. The effects of collective behavior on such issues as voting on a referendum or lobbying the city council induce citizens to seek out one another for cooperative action. Civic engagement is one avenue through which citizens can approach one another. Because they care about and have faith in the political valence of their voices, they will dare to trust others. When others reciprocate, the incentives for cooperation grow. Thus, trust and civic engagement, *in contexts that create the incentives for citizen cooperation,* reinforce one another. Clientelistic settings structured by vertical political networks create few incentives for citizens to

[19]Norris, *Critical Citizens;* Huntington, *The Third Wave.*

seek out one another in cooperative relationships. Donatella Della Porta captures these sentiments well; she writes, "Political corruption, in turn, reproduces this 'bad' social capital, rewarding those who belong to the 'right' networks and follow the 'right' norms."[20] As long as individuals can use their own merits to successfully access clientelistic networks, they do not require the collective efforts of their fellow citizens. Why join the PTO to work with other parents if I can change school policy by simply voicing my concern to a client of the state?

Another side of this cycle of trust and civic engagement captures the experiences of the democratic supporters in the West Bank. By becoming more civically engaged through their affiliation with anti-government associations, democrats' expectations for themselves—that they would be accorded the same rights and privileges as other democratic citizens across the globe—also implied that their expectations for what they would deem trustworthy characteristics had increased. Significantly, this trustworthiness did not include the eager promotion of interests through clientelistic channels. As a result, the problem of social trust was compounded for the democrats in the West Bank, becoming something of a vicious cycle. Democrats did not have the support of political institutions to serve and protect their trusting relations; they had higher standards for what constitutes a trustworthy relationship; they were more likely to recognize the abuses of the authoritarian regime; and they were more likely to have greater expectations of their fellow citizens. But these expectations remained unrealized, and the democrats' levels of social trust fell.

Being a strong supporter of democratic institutions in a nondemocratic setting meant that these citizens primarily felt that democratic institutions suited their everyday needs better than other types of ruling arrangements. They did not accord the regime in power deference simply because of its position but felt that government should communicate with, respond to, and represent all citizens. They believed that they deserved a relationship to their government that would recognize their citizenship, perhaps comparing their plight to that of millions of others who enjoy the rule of democratic governance.

Because democrats tended to fall outside the good graces of the PNA, they could not rely on government institutions to sanction those who might sever relationships based on trust. Because they—for good reason—had little faith in the government and believed that *all* citizens should work together to overcome the abuses of the regime, they sought the help of their fellow citizens, expecting them to be as disappointed and frustrated with the inadequacies of government as they were. But when more and more citizens became part of the PNA's clientelistic regime,

---

[20]Della Porta, "Social Capital," 205.

democrats were dealt a serious blow, and their levels of trust plummeted. Democrats saw those who involved themselves in patron-client relations as communal sellouts.[21] Levels of interpersonal distrust, then, are a positive indicator when we consider whether citizens desire, demand, and work for democratic reforms in a nondemocratic polity. Just as levels of trust can be good in some polities, so too can levels of distrust.[22]

## THE ART OF ASSOCIATION

> After the PNA came, the PNA fought the idea of community, because community is a power base. So it fought this. It wanted to create a new community under PNA [rule]. It employs over eighty thousand people. . . . We have to get people involved to address this.
> —Anti-PNA associational leader, 1999[23]

What do these findings tell us about associational life and the building blocks of a democratic polity? The potential democratic functions of associational life are multifaceted. My goal is not to discredit current theoretical gains but rather to add a layer of nuance and argue that things might just work differently in the developing world.

In this regard, we must ask ourselves what role associational life actually plays in these other, nondemocratic, areas of the world. Few associations in the West Bank formed for the sole purpose of democratization or democratic effectiveness. Some associations in the West Bank, like associations elsewhere, formed to fulfill basic communal functions: to create spaces where citizens could meet and engage with one another, where they could partake of specific programs, such as those of the Boy Scouts, the YWCA, or sports clubs. Associations like these have large and dynamic constituencies. But associations in the less democratic world also organized around specific programmatic initiatives focused on welfare and charity. Most associations in the West Bank have focused their efforts on charitable causes, and they are busy working to raise funds by creating products for sale or organizing community events. An obvious demand

---

[21]Those who enter patron-client relations and those who promote them need not necessarily see themselves as sellouts. In the words of Donatella Della Porta, "Corruption may be regarded as the way things work, and corrupt politicians as those who actually deliver the services and jobs—at least for their own constituencies" (ibid., 202).

[22]Hart, *Distrust and Democracy.*

[23]Amaney Jamal, interview with Palestinian anti-PNA association leader NAP, summer 1999.

for these types of services exists, as these services are not made readily available by state institutions. That these associations, including welfare associations, were susceptible to clientelistic outreach and co-optation by the state raises serious concerns about the usefulness of associations in producing democratic outcomes.

But to dismiss the important roles associational life plays would be to ignore the fact that many of these associations provide basic subsistence requirements to their members. An analysis of associational life and its potential impact on democratic developments within a given region needs to account for the overarching economic dynamics of poverty and need in these settings. Most casual observers of the Palestinian scene would perhaps have little problem dismissing my findings here about associational life's impact on democratic citizenship by simply pointing out that the charitable and welfare-promoting associations, however embedded they may be in clientelistic networks, provide key material and economic resources to a very needy population.[24] In the words of Tariq Ismael, "Civil formations have played a crucial role in maintaining the social fabric of society during crises. The existence of civil associations— in Lebanon during the civil war, 1975–90; in Palestine during the Intifada, in Kuwait during the Iraqi invasion and occupation, in Turkey after the 1999 earthquakes and the networks of contacts they create provide material and moral support to citizens both at home and abroad."[25] Talking about desirable citizenship qualities is nearly impossible without first addressing basic human material needs.

And yet one must not discount those associations that, more critical of the PNA, rejected the clientelistic networks. These associations were more impoverished and unable to compete with the programs offered by pro-PNA associations. How can we explain why some associations became PNA clients much more easily than others? Ideological commitments cannot capture the whole story. Many leaders in my sample explained that they did not necessarily endorse Fatah as a political party, or that they were at one point only halfhearted supporters of Oslo. But as time passed, these leaders—in great need of resources for their associations and members—became PNA supporters. The democrats in the West Bank exhibited higher expectations of what constitutes trustworthiness. They were more involved in and concerned about their local en-

---

[24]Other important functions, according to Mudar Kassis, include trying to establish democratic rights and procedures as well as training for leadership. Mudar Kassis, "Civil Society Organizations and Transition to Democracy in Palestine," *Voluntas: International Journal of Voluntary and Nonprofit Organizations* 12.1 (2001).

[25]Ismael, *Middle East Politics Today,* 73.

vironments. But they had very few channels to press for change, and even when minuscule opportunities arose for participation, they could not compete financially with supporters of the regime. Many of these democrats—those most skillful, as is typical in many other regions of the Middle East—ended up leaving for the West, fueling the drain of Palestinian intelligentsia. Some of those who stayed ended up in jail, while others continued to wait for the day when they too would enjoy the democratic rights that many citizens across the globe enjoy from birth.

## A NOTE ABOUT DEMOCRATIZATION

The implications of these findings for donor-oriented policies that aim to "educate" and "democratize" citizens at the grassroots level are considerable. Thus far, the findings of this investigation indicate that the polarized and state-centralized contexts of the West Bank and Morocco—and associational interactions within these contexts—override other key trust and democratic inducements, such as donor aid. Many a project focuses on how to increase and enhance the social capital of various peoples in the developing world through promoting and increasing associational life. The assumption driving these projects is that citizens enjoy sufficient autonomy to make demands on the state. In states dominated by ruling governments and patrimonial linkages, where states are deeply embedded within society, the bottom-up approach to democracy is seriously flawed. The assumption driving donor assistance programs maintains that for citizenries to enjoy the endowments of democratic rule they first must acquire the qualities of the "civic community," without which there can be no democracy. But these conclusions are based on studies with an important selection bias. Our understanding of civic engagement and interpersonal trust as desirable for democracy are derived from research based on Western democratic contexts. These studies need to take into account that the starting point for democracy in many a state in the developing world differs from that of earlier democratizers. State entrenchment and domination in developing societies need to be addressed within a larger developmental paradigm. In these contexts one questions the ability of civil society to disengage the state. Where disengagement occurs, alienation and marginalization ensue.

Political theorists, historians, and scholars must consider—in a variety of contexts—how civic-political institutional relations shape levels of interpersonal trust, civic engagement, and support for democratic institutions, as well as their usefulness to democratic outcomes. Only when studies make fine, informed distinctions about the consistency of the civic sector under investigation will they contribute a more accurate understanding of civil society in the developing world.

Special attention needs to be given to the fact that across Africa, the Middle East, Latin America, and Asia, states play more hegemonic roles in the daily affairs of their societies than in Western democratic countries. Therefore, civil society and the quality and form of civic engagement in these polities will be shaped by their overall contexts. Although this project explains the relationship between interpersonal trust and democracy in state-centralized settings, we still know little about how levels of interpersonal trust aid the journey toward democratization. Accompanying the current surge of model testing and scientific inquiry should be a set of causal explanations linking vibrant civil societies to paths of democratization in state-centralized societies. At the very minimum, this new body of literature should begin to explain the ways civil societies have been useful in state-dominated contexts. More attention should be drawn to the difference between empirical realities and theory. Further, very few studies have specifically looked at how democratic institutions—or the lack thereof—influence the quality and form of civic engagement. Seldom have studies focused on the "moving parts" of democratic or other forms of governance in shaping, promoting, and enhancing levels of civic engagement in ways that are supportive of democracy.

In an era where democracy in the Arab world lies heavy on the minds of analysts, policy makers and scholars, they are advised to take a serious look at the ways in which entrenched and embedded states have molded civil societies. Civil societies in the Arab world are not independent creations of preexisting civic orientations and beliefs. Today's Arab civil societies are constructions of decades-old authoritarian and state-centralized policies. If the hope is to promote civil society in ways effective for democracy, this underlying starting point needs to become the governing paradigm of analysis.

# Appendixes

DURING SIX MONTHS of field research in the West Bank, I gathered data from three different sources to test the proposition that associational life is related to civic engagement and civic attitudes supportive of democratic outcomes. In these data, I found evidence indicating that any assessment of the effect of associational life on individual attitudes and behaviors needs to take into account the overall political environment in which associations operate.[1] Using survey data and open-ended interviews of association leaders in the West Bank, I examined (1) the difference in attitudes between association members and nonassociation members, (2) the role association leaders play in mediating civic engagement, and (3) whether different types of associations promote varying levels and patterns of civic engagement and civic attitudes.[2]

The Jerusalem Media and Communications Center (JMCC) administered the first survey instrument, a random assessment of 1,200 Palestinians. This survey measured the differences in political participation patterns and civic attitudes of both members and nonmembers of civic associations in the West Bank. The second survey consisted of 422 association members in the West Bank. A more elaborate and extensive instrument, this second survey built on the JMCC survey. This survey gathered data on five basic dimensions of civic engagement and civic attitudes: (1) interpersonal trust, (2) support for democratic institutions, (3) community engagement, (4) degree of involvement in voluntary groups (civic involvement), and (5) political knowledge.[3]

I randomly sampled Palestinian civic associations from a comprehensive list of approximately 1,100 civic associations in the West Bank

---

[1] I spent three months in 1998 and three months in 1999.

[2] The collection of all survey data took place in PNA-controlled territories of the West Bank: areas A and B, but not C. During the interim period, the PNA obtained full control and sovereignty over 17% of the West Bank; this Palestinian-controlled area was designated area A. Area B, consisting of roughly 24% of the West Bank, is under joint Israeli-Palestinian rule. In area B, Palestinians are responsible for all civilian affairs, while Israel is responsible for security matters. Area C, the remaining 59% of the West Bank, remains under full Israeli control and jurisdiction.

[3] Questions were drawn from surveys that had already been used to measure levels of civic engagement elsewhere cross-nationally. I used survey questions that had been used by the NES, by Verba, Scholzman, and Brady in *Voice and Equality,* by Almond and Verba in *The Civic Culture,* by the Pew Survey on Trust, and by the Public Opinion Service surveys on democratic culture. In some cases, I modified questions so that they addressed the particularities of the Palestinian case.

including women's groups, charitable societies, sports clubs, and youth associations. I obtained this list from the Birzeit Research Center in Ramallah.[4] Visiting over one hundred sites, I carried out over sixty open-ended ethnographic interviews with associational leaders, observing their organizational functions in Ramallah, Nablus, Hebron, Bethlehem, East Jerusalem, Tulkarem, and the surrounding villages. I asked leaders a series of questions about their associations, the role of the leaders in the association, why leaders were involved, the types of programs within their associations, and the relationship between the different associations and the PNA. Though some leaders were comfortable speaking in English, I administered the majority of interviews in Arabic. Of over sixty association leaders I initially interviewed, only forty-two qualified for the data analysis of this study.[5] I randomly sampled ten to fifteen members from each of the forty-two associations included in this study. This sample of association members answered a survey instrument prepared in Arabic to obtain information on civic attitudes, behaviors, and activities. The associations in this study represent areas from across the West Bank, and pertinent control variables include source of funding, socioeconomic status, and proximity to the PNA.

[4]Because the Law of Associations had not been ratified in 1999, civic associations in the West Bank and Gaza were not required to register with any government office. As a result, some associations obtained licensing from the Ministry of Social Affairs, others from the Ministry of the Interior, and yet others at the Ministry of Justice. Once the Law of Associations was passed during August of 1999, civic associations were to register with the Ministry of the Interior. Owing to these circumstances, I was unable to obtain a comprehensive list of licensed associations from any government office. However, the list I did obtain was far more comprehensive than any of the other independent lists I gathered from the ministries, UN offices, and various other research NGOs.

[5]The remaining associations not included in this study did not have sufficient membership for this study or did not operate in PNA-controlled areas. Qualifications for membership included frequent attendance requirements and fee payment, and being a member gave one the right to vote within the association.

# Survey Questions and Coding
# of Association Members

A) INTERPERSONAL TRUST (INDEX VARIABLE CONSISTING

OF THREE QUESTIONS) (CRONBACH'S ALPHA: .76)

1) Help Others: Do you feel you have an obligation to help others in your community?
   a) Yes, a lot
   b) A little
   c) No, not really
   d) No opinion
2) Trust Others: Would you say that most of the time people try to be helpful or that they are mostly looking out for themselves?
   a) Yes, most people are helpful
   b) No, they try to look out only for themselves
   c) No opinion
3) Take Advantage: Do you think most people would try to take advantage of you if they got a chance or would they try to be fair?
   a) Yes, most people would take advantage of me
   b) No, they try to be fair
   c) No opinion

*Coding: 4 point additive scale from 0 to 4. Low interpersonal trust coded as 0 and 1, high interpersonal trust coded as 3 and 4.*

| Interpersonal Trust: | |
|---|---|
| Low trust | 67.93% |
| High trust | 32.07% |
| *N* | 368 |

B) SUPPORT FOR DEMOCRATIC INSTITUTIONS (INDEX

VARIABLE CONSISTING OF NINE QUESTIONS)

(CRONBACH'S ALPHA .89)

1) Parties: Establishment of political parties should always be guaranteed to everyone.
   a) Yes, I agree

    b) No, I disagree
    c) I don't know
2) Law: The PNA is justified in breaking the constitution.
    a) Yes, I agree
    b) No, I disagree
    c) I don't know
3) Judicial Independence: The judicial system must be independent.
    a) Yes, I agree
    b) No, I disagree
    c) I don't know
4) Impeachment: It should be possible for the parliament to impeach the president.
    a) Yes, I agree
    b) No, I disagree
    c) I don't know
5) Election: High officials should be elected.
    a) Important
    b) Somewhat important
    c) Not important
    d) No opinion
6) Opposition Rights: Maintenance of the opposition rights.
    a) Important
    b) Somewhat important
    c) Not important
    d) No opinion
7) Constitutional Limits: Constitutional restrictions on the government.
    a) Important
    b) Somewhat important
    c) Not important
    d) No opinion
8) Free Elections: Free and fair elections.
    a) Important
    b) Somewhat important
    c) Not important
    d) No opinion
9) Free Speech: Complete freedom to criticize government.
    a) Important
    b) Somewhat important
    c) Not important
    d) No opinion

*Coding: Additive scale from high to low (0–11). Actual scale 7–11. Coding 7–9 (lower), 10–11 (higher).*

Support for Democratic Institutions:
Lower support     43.13%
Higher support    56.87%
N                 364

## C) COMMUNITY ENGAGEMENT (INDEX VARIABLE CONSISTING OF TWO QUESTIONS)

1) Local Discussions: How often do you usually discuss local community problems with others in this community?
   a) Every day
   b) At least once a week
   c) Less than once a week
   d) I don't know
2) Care: Do you think your interest in local community affairs has increased, decreased, or stayed the same since you joined this association?
   a) Increased a lot
   b) Increased a little
   c) Remained the same
   d) Decreased a little
   e) Decreased a lot
   f) I don't know

*Coding: Additive scale from low to high (0–4). Collapsed 0–2 (low), 3–4 (high).*

Community Engagement:
Lower political engagement     39.71%
Higher political engagement    60.29%
N                              345

## D) CIVIC INDEX (INDEX VARIABLE CONSISTING OF FIVE QUESTIONS) (CRONBACH'S ALPHA .79)

1) Vote: Do you vote in your association?
   a) Yes
   b) No
   c) I don't know
2) Discussions: Do you discuss issues within your association?
   a) Yes
   b) No
   c) I don't know

3) Organize: Do you organize meetings and events in your association?
   a) Yes
   b) No
   c) I don't know
4) Speech: Do you give speeches in your association?
   a) Yes
   b) No
   c) I don't know
5) Workshops: Do you participate in workshops and seminars in your association?
   a) Yes
   b) No
   c) I don't know

*Coding: Additive scale (0–4) from low to high: 0–2 (low), 3–4(high).*

|  | Civic Index: |
|---|---|
| Low | 48.38% |
| High | 51.62% |
| *N* | 370 |

E) POLITICAL KNOWLEDGE (INDEX VARIABLE CONSISTING OF FOUR QUESTIONS) (CRONBACH'S ALPHA .61)

1) Representatives: Do you know two local representatives?
   a) Yes (provide names)
   b) No
   c) I don't know
2) Interest: How do you evaluate your overall interest in politics?
   a) Very interested
   b) Somewhat interested
   c) Not interested
   d) No opinion
3) Read Newspapers: How many times do you read the newspaper per week?
   a) None
   b) Once
   c) Twice
   d) Three times
   e) Four times

    f) Five+
    g) No opinion
4) Listen to the News: How many times do you listen to the news daily?
    a) None
    b) Once
    c) Twice
    d) Three times
    e) Four times
    f) Five+
    g) No opinion

*Coding: Additive score from low to high: 0–8. Actual results 2–8. Variable collapsed into two categories: 2–5 (low), 6–8 (high).*

Political Knowledge:

| | |
|---|---|
| Low political knowledge | 34.35% |
| High political knowledge | 65.65% |
| N | 294 |

## F) PNA EVALUATION (INDEX VARIABLE CONSISTING OF FOUR QUESTIONS) (CRONBACH'S ALPHA: .66)

1) Palestinian Legislative Council: Looking back to the last three years since the Palestinian National Council has been elected, what is your opinion about its performance in general? Would you say you are:
    a) Very dissatisfied
    b) Dissatisfied
    c) Satisfied
    d) Very satisfied
    e) I don't know
2) Corruption: Some Palestinians think that the level of corruption in the Palestinian National Authority is high; others think that there is corruption, but it is not widespread; still others think there isn't any corruption. What do you think?
    a) No corruption
    b) There is corruption, but it is not widespread
    c) Corruption is high
    d) No opinion
3) Fear: In your opinion, can the people of Palestine criticize the Palestinian National Authority without fear?
    a) Yes

      b) No
      c) No opinion
    4) Fair: Do you think the police around here treat all citizens equally, or do they give some people better treatment than others?
      a) Give some people better treatment than others
      b) Treat people equally
      c) No opinion

*Coding: Additive scale from low to high (0–9 scale, actual scale 0–3). Variable collapsed into two categories: 0–1 (low support), 2–3 (high support).*

| PNA Evaluation: | |
| --- | --- |
| Low evaluation | 82.33% |
| High evaluation | 17.67% |
| *N* | 294 |

### G) OPEN-ENDED QUESTIONS OF ASSOCIATION LEADERS

    1) Support of PNA: How would you describe your relationship with the PNA? *Coding: percentage of members in PNA-supporting associations. 1 = no relationship, just formalities. 2 = good/very good relationship.*

| Support of PNA: | |
| --- | --- |
| No relationship | 48.62% |
| Good/very good relationship | 51.38% |
| *N* | 399 |

### H) GENDER

| Female (1) | 53.08% |
| --- | --- |
| Male (2) | 46.92% |
| *N* | 422 |

### J) EDUCATION

| Less than high school (1) | 9.77% |
| --- | --- |
| High school (2) | 34.34% |
| High school and above (3) | 55.89% |
| *N* | 399 |

### K) AGE

Continuous variable

# Survey Questions and Coding of General Palestinian Population

## A) NGO MEMBERS

In our society, there are a large number of civil organizations (non-governmental) like the charitable associations, trade unions, and the youth organizations like clubs, the developmental organizations that provide services in health and agriculture. Also, the research centers, women's centers, human rights centers, and any nongovernmental organization. Are you a member in any of these organizations?

|  |  |
|---|---|
| Yes (1) | 19.73% |
| No (0) | 80.27% |
| N | 1,166 |

## B) WORK

Do you work?

|  |  |
|---|---|
| Yes (1) | 44.78% |
| No (0) | 55.22% |
| N | 1,197 |

## C) GENDER

|  |  |
|---|---|
| Female (1) | 54.38% |
| Male (2) | 45.62% |
| N | 1,199 |

## D) FACTION (FATAH)

What is the political faction you mostly trust?

|  |  |
|---|---|
| Fatah (1) | 32.15% |
| Non-Fatah (0) | 67.85% |
| N | 1,042 |

## E) AGE

Continuous variable

## F) SUPPORT FOR OSLO PEACE PROCESS (ONE QUESTION)

1) In general, what do you feel toward the Israeli-Palestinian Peace Process?
   a) Strongly support
   b) Somewhat support
   c) Neither support nor oppose
   d) Somewhat oppose
   e) Strongly oppose
   f) No answer

| | |
|---|---|
| Support Oslo: (1) | 59.04% |
| Do not support Oslo (0) | 40.96% |
| $N$ | 1,172 |

## G) EDUCATION:

| | |
|---|---|
| Elementary (1) | 12.66% |
| Preparatory (2) | 22.39% |
| Secondary (3) | 33.51% |
| Some college (4) | 22.31% |
| College and above (5) | 9.13% |
| $N$ | 1,161 |

## H) SOCIAL TRUST

1) In your opinion, do you feel that most people now like to be useful to others or most of them care about their own personal interests?
   a) Most people would like to help others
   b) Most people care about their own personal interests
   c) Nearly half the people care about their own personal interests while the other half care about others
   d) I don't know
2) Do you feel that you are obliged to help others in your society?
   a) Yes
   b) No
   c) I don't know

*Coding: Additive scale (1–3).*

| Social Trust: | |
|---|---|
| Low trust | 11.28% |
| Medium trust | 59.42% |
| High trust | 29.30% |
| $N$ | 1,172 |

I) PNA EVALUATION (5 QUESTIONS) (CRONBACH'S ALPHA .79)

1) In general, how do you evaluate the performance of the Legislative Council?
   a) Very good
   b) Good
   c) Bad
   d) Very bad

2) In general, how do you evaluate the performance of the Palestinian Authority?
   a) Very good
   b) Good
   c) Bad
   d) Very bad
   e) I don't know

3) How do you evaluate the role of the judicial system in Palestine?
   a) Very good
   b) Good
   c) Bad
   d) Very bad
   e) I don't know

4) What do you think of the Palestinian security apparatuses?
   a) Very good
   b) Good
   c) Bad
   d) Very bad
   e) I don't know

5) In your opinion, what is the extent of corruption (if found) in the Palestinian Authority apparatuses or institutions?
   a) Widely spread
   b) Somewhat spread
   c) A little spread
   d) Not spread at all

*Coding: Additive scale (0–14), lower evaluation (0); higher evaluation (1). (0–8 low, 9–14 High).*

| | |
|---|---|
| Lower PNA evaluation: (0) | 42.43% |
| Higher PNA evaluation (1) | 57.57% |
| N | 1,011 |

# Survey Questions and Coding of General Moroccan Population (World Values Survey Questions)

## A) INTERPERSONAL TRUST

1) Generally speaking, would you say that most people can be trusted or that most people cannot be trusted?
   a) Most people can be trusted
   b) Most people cannot be trusted
   c) Do not know

Morocco:

| | |
|---|---|
| Most people cannot be trusted (0) | 77.18% |
| Most people can be trusted (1) | 22.82% |
| $N$ | 2,200 |

## B) SUPPORT FOR DEMOCRACY (INDEX VARIABLE CONSISTING OF TWO QUESTIONS)

1) Support for Democracy: Democracy may have problems, but it's better than any other form of government.
   a) Agree strongly
   b) Agree
   c) Disagree
   d) Strongly disagree
2) Support for democratic system: I am going to describe various types of political systems and ask what you think about each as a way of governing your country. For each one, would you say it is a very good, fairly good, fairly bad, or very bad way of governing this country?
   a) Very good
   b) Fairly good
   c) Fairly bad
   d) Very bad

*Coding: High support = 1; mild support–No support at all = 0.*

Morocco:

| | |
|---|---|
| Lower democratic support (0) | 28.38% |
| High democratic support (1) | 71.62% |
| *N* | 1,392 |

## C) POLITICAL CONFIDENCE (TWO QUESTIONS)

1) Political Confidence: I am going to name a number of organizations. For each one could you tell me how much confidence you have in it: a great deal of confidence, quite a lot of confidence, not very much confidence, or none at all.
   a) The government
2) Political Confidence: I am going to name a number of organizations. For each one could you tell me how much confidence you have in it: a great deal of confidence, quite a lot of confidence, not very much confidence, or none at all.
   a) Parliament

*Coding: Additive scale (1–7): 1–4, low confidence; 5–7, high confidence.*

Morocco:

| | |
|---|---|
| Low confidence(0) | 56.69% |
| High confidence (1) | 43.31% |
| *N* | 1,785 |

# Bibliography

Abu 'Amr, Ziad. "Pluralism and Palestinians." *Journal of Democracy* 7 (1996).
———. Al-Mujtama al-madani wa-al-tahawul al-dimmuqrati al-Filastini (*Civil Society and Democratic Change in Palestinian Society.*) Ramallah: Muwatin, 1995.

Almond, Gabriel, and Sidney Verba. *The Civic Culture: Political Attitudes and Democracy in Five Nations.* Princeton: Princeton UP, 1963.

Anderson, Lisa. "Democracy in the Arab World: A Critique of the Political Culture Approach." In *Political Liberalization and Democratization in the Arab World.* Ed. Rex Brynen, Bahgat Korany, and Paul Noble. Vol. 1. Boulder: Lynne Rienner, 1995.

———. "Peace and Democracy in the Middle East: The Constraints of Soft Budgets." *Journal of International Affairs* (Summer 1985).

Anoushiravan, Ehteshami, and Emma Murphy. "Transformation of the Corporatist State in the Middle East." *Third World Quarterly* 17.4 (1996).

Ashrawi, Hanan. "Lawlessness and the Rule of Law." *Media Monitors* (20 Jan. 2001, 27 July 2002). http://www.mediamonitors.net/hanan10.html.

Auyero, Javier. "'From the Client's Point(s) of View': How Poor People Perceive and Evaluate Political Clientelism." *Theory and Society* 28 (1999).

Baaklini, Abdo, Guilain Denoeux, and Robert Springborg. *Legislative Politics in the Arab World: The Resurgence of Democratic Institutions.* Boulder: Lynne Rienner, 1999.

Beck, Martin. "The External Dimensions of Authoritarian Rule in Palestine." *Journal of International Relations and Development* 3.1 (2000).

Bellin, Eva. "Contingent Democrats: Industrialists, Labor, and Democratization in Late-Developing Countries." *World Politics* 52.2 (Jan. 2000).

———. "The Robustness of Authoritarianism in the Middle East: Exceptionalism in Comparative Perspective." *Comparative Politics* 36.2 (Jan. 2004).

Bendourou, Omar. "Power and Opposition in Morocco," *Journal of Democracy* 7.3 (1996).

Bergman, Ronen. "How Much PA Corruption Is Too Much?" *Haaretz* 19 (Oct. 1999).

Berman, Sherri. "Civil Society and the Collapse of the Weimar Republic." *World Politics* 49.3 (Apr. 1997).

Bermeo, Nancy, and Philip Nord, eds. "Civil Society after Democracy: Some Conclusions." In *Civil Society Before Democracy: Lessons From Nineteenth-Century Europe.* New York: Rowan and Littlefield, 2000.

Bianchi, Robert. *Unruly Corporatism: Associational Life in Twentieth-Century Egypt.* Oxford: Oxford UP, 1989.

Bisharah, Azmi. *Musahama i Naqd al-Mujtam'a al-Madani (Pursuit in the Critique of Civil Society).* West Bank: Ramallah, 1996.

Blair, Harry. "Donors, Democratization and Civil Society: Relating Theory to Practice." In *NGO State and Donors*. Ed. David Hulme and Michael Edwards. New York: St. Martin's Press, 1970.

Braithwaite, Valeria, and Margaret Levi, eds. *Trust and Governance*. New York: Russell Sage Foundation, 1998.

Brand, Laurie. "'In the Beginning Was the State . . .': The Quest for Civil Society in Jordan." In *Civil Society in the Middle East*. ed. Augustus Richard Norton, New York: E.J. Brill, 1996. 115–16, 166–67, 176.

———. "Displacement for Development? The Impact of Changing State-Society Relations." *World Development* (June 2001).

———. "The Intifadah and the Arab World: Old Players, New Roles." *International Journal* (1990).

———. *Palestinians in the Arab World: Institution Building and Search for State*. New York: Columbia UP, 1988.

Bratton, Michael, and Nicolas van de Walle. *Democratic Experiments in Africa: Regime Transition in Comparative Perspective*. Cambridge: Cambridge UP, 1997.

Brehm, John, and Wendy Rahn. "Individual-Level Evidence for the Causes and Consequences of Social Capital." *American Journal of Political Science* (July 1997).

Brown, Nathan. "Constituting Palestine: The Effort to Write a Basic Law for the Palestinian Authority." *Middle East Journal* 54 (2000).

———. *Palestinian Politics after the Oslo Accords: Resuming Arab Palestine*. Berkeley: U of California Press, 2003.

Brownlee, Jason. "The Decline of Pluralism in Mubarak's Egypt." *Journal of Democracy* 13.4 (2002).

Brynen, Rex. "The Dynamics of Palestinian Elite Formation." *Journal of Palestine Studies* (Spring 1995).

———. "The Neo-patrimonial Dimension to Palestinian Politics." *Journal of Palestine Studies* (Autumn 1995).

———. *A Very Political Economy: Peace Building and Foreign Aid in the West Bank and Gaza*. Washington, DC: United States Institute of Peace Press, 2000.

Brynen, Rex. "From Occupation to Uncertainty: Palestine." In *Political Liberalization and Democratization in the Arab World*. Eds. Rex Brynen, Baghat Korany, and Paul Noble. Vol. 2. Colorado: Lynne Rienner, 1998.

Brynen, Rex, Baghat Korany, and Paul Noble, eds. *Political Liberalization and Democratization in the Arab World: Theoretical Perspectives*. Boulder: Lynne Rienner, 1995.

Butenschon, Nils, Uri Davis, and Manuel Hassassian, eds. *Citizenship and the State in the Middle East: Approaches and Applications*. Syracuse: Syracuse UP, 2000.

Carapico, Shelia. "Foreign Aid for Promoting Democracy in the Arab World." *Middle East Journal* 53.1 (2000).

Chazan, Naomi. "Engaging the State: Associational Life in Sub-Saharan Africa." In *State Power and Social Forces: Domination and Transformation in the Third World*. Eds. Joel Migdal, Atul Kohli, and Vivienne Shue. Cambridge: Cambridge UP, 1994.

Chhibber, Pradeep, and Samuel Eldersveld. "Local Elites and Popular Support for Economic Reform in China and India." *Comparative Political Studies* 33:3 (2000).

Chhibber, Pradeep, and Mariano Torcal. "Elite Strategy, Social Cleavages, and Party Systems in a New Democracy." *Comparative Political Studies* 30:1 (1997).

Clark, Janine. *Islam, Charity and Activism: Middle-Class Networks and Social Activism in Egypt, Jordan and Yemen.* Bloomington: Indiana UP, 2004.

Clark, John. "The State, Popular Participation, and the Voluntary Sector." *World Development* 32:4 (1995).

Cohen, Joshua, and Joel Rogers. *Associations and Democracy.* New York: Verso, 1995.

———. "Secondary Associations and Democratic Governance." *Politics and Society* 20 (1992).

Coleman, James. *The Foundation of Social Theory.* Cambridge: Harvard UP, 1990.

Cook, Karen, ed. *Trust in Society.* New York: Russell Sage Foundation, 2003.

Craig, Jeffrey. "Caste, Class, and Clientelism: A Political Economy of Everyday Corruption in Rural North India." *Economic Geography* (Jan. 2002).

Cunningham, Karla J. "Factors Influencing Jordan's Information Revolution: Implications for Democracy." *Middle East Journal* 56.2 (2002).

Davis, Uri. *Citizenship and the State: A Comparative Study of Citizenship Legislation in Israel, Jordan, Palestine, Syria and Lebanon.* New York: Ithaca Press, 1997.

"Defying the Rule of Law: Political Detainees Held without Charge or Trial." *Amnesty International.* Retrieved 21 Apr. 1999, 27 July 2002. http://web.amnesty.org/802568F7005C4453/0/3762B4D74B169F928025690000692C22?Open.

Della Porta, Donatella. "Social Capital, Beliefs in Government, and Political Corruption." In *Disaffected Democracies: What's Troubling the Trilateral Countries?* Ed. Susan Pharr and Robert Putnam. Princeton, NJ: Princeton UP, 2000.

Denoeux, Guilain. "Morocco's Economic Prospects: Daunting Challenges Ahead." *Middle East Policy* 8 (June 2001).

———. "The Politics of Morocco's 'Fight against Corruption.'" *Middle East Policy Council* 8.2 (2000).

Denoeux, Guilain, and Abdeslam Maghraoui. "King Hassan's Strategy of Political Dualism." *Middle East Policy* (Jan. 1998).

Diamond, Larry, Juan Linz, and Seymour Martin Lipset. "What Makes for Democracy?" In *Politics in Developing Countries: Comparing Experiences with Democracy.* Ed. Larry Diamond, Juan Linz, and Seymour Martin Lipset. 2nd ed. Boulder: Lynne Rienner, 1995.

Diamond, Larry, and Marc Plattner, eds. "Toward Democratic Consolidation." In *The Global Resurgence of Democracy.* Ed. Larry Diamond and Marc Plattner. 2nd ed. Baltimore: The John Hopkins UP, 1996.

Domingo, Pilar. "Judicial Independence and Judicial Reform in Latin America." In *The Self-Restraining State.* Ed. Andreas Schedler, Larry Diamond, and Marc Palttner. Boulder: Lynne Rienner, 1999.

Edwards, Bob, Michael Foley, and Mario Diani, eds. *Beyond Tocqueville: Civil Society and the Social Capital Debate in Comparative Perspective.* New England: Tufts UP, 2001.

Eldersveld, Samuel. *Political Elites in Modern Societies.* Ann Arbor: The U of Michigan Press, 1989.

El-Glaoui, Halima. "Contributing to a Culture of Debate in Morocco." *Journal of Democracy* 10.1 (1999).

Evans, Peter. "The Eclipse of the State? Reflections on Stateness in an Era of Globalization." *World Politics* 50:1 (1997).

Farjoun, Emanuel. "Palestinian Workers in Israel—a Reserve Army of Labour." *Khamsin* 7 (1980).

Finkel, Steven. "Can Democracy Be Taught?" *Journal of Democracy* 14.4 (2003).

Foley, Michael, and Bob Edwards. "The Paradox of Civil Society." *Journal of Democracy* (July 1996).

Fox, Jonathan. "The Difficult Transition from Clientelism to Citizenship: Lessons from Mexico." *World Politics* 46.2 (Jan. 1994).

Freedom House. "Egypt." *Freedom in the World* (2003): 4–5. Retrieved 15 Sept. 2003. http://www.freedomhouse.org/research/freeworld/2003/countryratings/ egypt.htm. See also ratings for 2002 and 2004.

Frisch, Hilel, and Menachem Hofnung. "State Formation and International Aid: The Emergence of the Palestinian Authority." *World Development* 25:8 (1997).

Fukuyama, Francis. *The Great Disruption: Human Nature and the Reconstitution of Social Order.* New York: The Free Press, 1999.

———. "Social Capital." In *Culture Matters: How Values Shape Human Progress.* Eds. Lawrence Harrison and Samuel Huntington. New York: Basic Books, 2000.

———. "Social Capital, Civil Society, and Development." *Third World Quarterly* 22.1 (Feb. 2001).

———. *Trust: The Social Virtues and The Creation of Prosperity.* New York: Simon and Schuster, 1995.

Fullinwider, Robert, ed. *Civil Society, Democracy, and Civic Renewal.* New York: Rowman and Littlefield, 1999.

Fung, Archung. "Associations and Democracy: Between Theories, Hopes, and Realities." *Annual Review of Sociology* 29 (2003).

Giacaman, George. "In the Throes of Oslo: Palestinian Society, Civil Society and the Future." In *After Oslo: New Realities, Old Problems.* Ed. George Giacaman and Dag Jorund Lonning. Chicago: Pluto Press, 1998.

———. "The Role of Palestinian NGOs in the Development of Palestinian Civil Society." Unpublished paper. Mowatin, Ramallah, 1998.

Gibson, James. "Social Networks, Civil Society and the Prospects for Consolidating Russia's Democratic Transition." *American Journal of Political Science.* 45.1 (2001).

Gill, Graeme. *The Dynamics of Democratization: Elites, Civil Society and the Transition Process.* New York: St. Martin's Press, 2000.

Goldberg, Ellis, Resat Kasba, and Joel Migdal, eds. *Rules and Rights in the Middle East: Democracy Law and Society.* Seattle: U of Washington Press, 1993.

Haddadi, Said. "Two Cheers for Whom? The European Union and Democratization in Morocco." *Democratization* 9.1 (2002).

Hadi, Mahdi Abdul. "Decentralized Cooperation: Complement or Substitute to State-State-Cooperation?" Paper presented for the Research Group of European Affairs. U of Munich, February 1997.

Hagopian, Frances. "Traditional Politics against State Transformation in Brazil." In *State Power and Social Forces: Domination and Transformation in the Third*

*World.* Ed. Joel Migdal, Atul Kohli, and Vivienne Shue. Cambridge: Cambridge UP, 1994.

Hamarneh, Mustafa Mashru'. *al-Mujtama' al-madani wa-al-tahawwul al-Dimuqrati fi al-Watan al-'Arabi (The Civil Society Program and Democratic Transition in the Arab World).* Cairo: Ibn Khaldoun Center, 1995.

Hammami, Rema. "NGOs: The Professionalisation of Politics." *Race & Class* 37.2 (1995).

———. "Palestinian NGOs since Oslo: From NGO Politics to Social Movements?" *Middle East Report* 214 (Spring 2000).

Hammami, Reema, and Salim Tamari. "The Second Uprising: End or New Beginning?" *Journal of Palestine Studies* (Winter 2001).

Hamzeh, Nizar. "Clientelism, Lebanon: Roots and Trends." *Middle Eastern Studies* (July 2001).

Hardin, Russell. *Trust and Trustworthiness.* New York: Russell Sage, 2002.

Hart, Vivienne. *Distrust and Democracy: Political Distrust in Britain and America?* Cambridge: Cambridge UP 1978.

Hawthorne, Amy. "Middle Eastern Democracy: Is Civil Society the Answer?" *Carnegie Papers* (March 2004.)

Hearn, Julie. "Aiding Democracy? Donors and Civil Society in South Africa." *Third World Quarterly* 21.5 (2000).

Henderson, Sarah. *Building Democracy in Contemporary Russia.* Cornell: Cornell UP, 2003.

Hilal, Jamil. *al-Nizam al-Siyyasi al-Filistini ba'd Uslu (The Political Organizing Principles after Oslo).* Ramallah: Muwatin, 1998.

———. "State-Society Dynamics under the PNA." Ibn Khaldun Center. Retrieved Sept. 2000. http://www.ibnkhaldoun.org/newsletter/1999.

Hiltermann, Joost. *Behind the Intifada: Labor and Women's Movements in the Occupied Territories.* Princeton: Princeton UP, 1991.

Hoogh, Marc, and Dietland Stolle, eds. *Generating Social Capital: Civil Society and Institutions in Comparative Perspective.* New York: Palgrave Macmillan, 2003.

Howe, Marvine. *Morocco: The Islamist Awakening and Other Challenges.* New York: Oxford UP, 2005.

Huckfeldt, Robert, Eric Plutzer, and John Sprague. "Alternative Contexts of Political Behavior: Churches, Neighborhoods, and Individuals." *Journal of Politics* 55.2 (1993).

Hudock, Ann. *NGOs and Civil Society: Democracy by Proxy?* MA: Blackwell Publishers, 1999.

Huntington, Samuel. *Political Order in Changing Societies.* New Haven: Yale UP, 1968.

———. *The Third Wave: Democratization in the Late Twentieth Century.* Norman: U of Oklahoma Press, 1993.

Hutchcroft, Paul. "The Politics of Privilege: Assessing the Impact of Rents, Corruption, and Clientelism on Third World Development." *Political Studies* 45 (1997).

Ibrahim, Saad Eddin. "Crises, Elites and Democratization in the Arab World." *Middle East Journal* 47.2 (1993).

Ibrahim, Saad Eddin. "Democratization in the Arab World." In *Toward Civil Society in the Middle East? A Primer.* Ed. Jillian Schwedler. Boulder: Lynne Rienner, 1995.

———. "The Future of Civil Society in the Middle East." In *Toward Civil Society In the Middle East? A Primer.* Ed. Jillian Schwedler. Boulder: Lynne Rienner, 1995.

———. *al-Mujtama' wa-al-dawlah fi al-Watan al-'Arabi (Society and the State in the Arab World).* Beirut: Markaz Dirasat al-Wihda al-Arabiyya, 1988.

———. "Reform and Frustration in Egypt." In *Journal of Democracy* 7.4 (1996).

———. "A Reply to My Accusers." *Journal of Democracy* 11.4 (Oct. 2000).

Inglehart, Ronald. *Culture Shift in Advanced Industrial Society.* Princeton: Princeton UP, 1990.

Ismael, Tariq. *Middle East Politics Today: Government and Civil Society.* Gainesville: UP of Florida, 2001.

Jabbra, Joseph, and Nancy Jabbra. "Corruption and the Lack of Accountability in the Middle East." In *Where Corruption Lives.* Ed. Gerald E. Caiden, O. P. Dwivedi, and Joseph Jabbra. Conn.: Kumarian Press, 2001.

Jad, Islah, Penny Johnson, and Rita Giacaman. "Transit Citizens." In *Gender and Citizenship in the Middle East.* Ed. Joseph Suad. Syracuse: Syracuse UP, 2000.

Jamal, Amal. "State Building and Media Regime: Censoring the Emerging Public Sphere in Palestine." *Gazette* 63 (2001).

———. "State-Building, Institutionalization and Democracy: The Palestinian Experience." *Mediterranean Politics* (Autumn 2001).

Jamal, Manal. "After the Peace Processes: Foreign Donor Assistance and the Political Economy of Marginalization in Palestine and El Salvador." Ph.D. dissertation, McGill University, Spring, 2006.

Jresiat, Jamil. *Politics without Process: Administering Development in the Arab World.* Boulder: Lynne Rienner, 1997.

Key, V. O. *Public Opinion and American Democracy.* New York: Knopf, 1961.

Khalaf, Issa. *Politics in Palestine: Arab Factionalism and Social Disintegration, 1939–1948.* New York: Suny Press, 1991.

Khalifa, Aymen M. "Reviving Civil Society in Egypt." *Journal of Democracy* 6.3 (1995).

Kitschelt, Herbert. "Linkages between Citizens and Politicians in Democratic Polities." *Comparative Political Studies* 33.6–7 (Aug./Sept. 2000).

Kohli, Atul. "Centralization and Powerlessness: India's Democracy in a Comparative Perspective." In *State Power and Social Forces: Domination and Transformation in the Third World.* Ed. Joel Migdal, Atul Kohli, and Vivienne Shue. Cambridge: Cambridge UP, 1994.

Korany, Bahgat. "Restricted Democratization from Above: Egypt." In *Political Liberalization and Democratization in the Arab World.* Ed. Bahgat Korany, Rex Brynen, and Paul Noble. Vol. 2. Boulder: Lynne Rienner, 1998.

Krishna, Anirudh. "Enhancing Political Participation in Democracies: What Is the Role of Social Capital?" *Comparative Political Studies* 35.4 (2002).

Lane, Robert. *Political Life: Why and How People Get Involved in Politics.* New York: Basic Books, 1981.

LAW. "Executive Interference in the Palestinian Judiciary." In *The Palestinian*

*Society for the Protection of Human Rights and the Environment.* A report by the Independent Judiciary Unit, Apr. 1999.

Layachi, Azzedine. "Reform and Politics of Inclusion in the Maghreb." *Journal of North African Studies* 5.3.

———. *State, Society and Democracy in Morocco: The Limits of Associative Life.* Washington, DC: Center for Contemporary Arab Studies, Georgetown University, 1998.

Lesch, Mosley Ann. *Arab Politics in Palestine.* New York: Cornell UP, 1979.

———. *Transition to Palestinian Self-Government: Practical Steps Toward Israeli-Palestinian Peace.* Bloomington: Indiana UP, 1992.

Letki, Natalia. "Socialization for Participation? Trust, Membership, and Democratization in East-Central Europe." *Political Research Quarterly* 57.4 (2004).

Levi, Margaret. "Making Democracy Work: Book Review." *Politics and Society* 24 (1996).

Lin, Nan. *Social Capital: A Theory of Social Structure and Action.* Cambridge: Cambridge UP, 2001.

Linz, Juan, and Alfred Stepan. *Problems of Democratic Transition and Consolidation: Southern Europe, South America and Post-communist Europe.* Maryland: The John Hopkins UP, 1996.

Lonning, Dag Jorund. "Vision and Reality Diverging: Palestinian Survival Strategies in the Post-Oslo Era." In *After Oslo: New Realities, Old Problems.* Ed. George Giacaman and Dag Jorund Lonning. Chicago: Pluto Press, 1998.

Lowrance, Sherry R. "After Beijing: Political Liberalization and the Women's Movement in Jordan." *Middle Eastern Studies* 34.3 (1998).

Lucas, Russell. "Deliberalization in Jordan." *Journal of Democracy* 4.1 (2003).

Lupia, Arthur, and Mathew McCubbins. *The Democratic Dilemma: Can Citizens Learn What They Need To Know?* Cambridge: Cambridge UP, 1998.

Lust-Okar, Ellen M. "The Decline of Jordanian Political Parties: Myth of Reality?" *International Journal of Middle Eastern Studies* 33 (2001).

———. *Structuring Conflict in the Arab World: Incumbents, Opponents, and Institutions.* Cambridge: Cambridge UP, 2005.

Maghraoui, Abdeslam. "Democratization in the Arab World: Depolitization in Morocco." *Journal of Democracy* 13.4 (2002).

———. "Monarchy and Political Reform in Morocco." *Journal of Democracy* 12.1 (2001).

———. "Political Authority in Crisis." *Middle East Report* (Spring 2001).

May, Rachel and Andrew Milton, eds. *(Un)civil Societies: Human Rights and Democratic Transitions in Eastern Europe and Latin America.* Oxford: Lexington Books, 2005.

Mazawi, Elias Andre, and Abraham Yogev. "Elite Formation under Occupation: The Internal Stratification of Palestinian Elites in the West Bank and Gaza Strip." *British Journal of Sociology* (Sept. 1999).

McDowell, David. *The Palestinians: The Road to Nationhood.* London: Minority Rights Publications, 1994.

MIFTAH (Palestinian Initiative for the Promotion of Global Dialogue and Democracy). http://www.miftah.org/Display.cfm?DocId=82&CategoryId=4.

Migdal, Joel. *Palestinian Society and Politics.* Princeton: Princeton UP, 1980.

Migdal, Joel. *State in Society: Studying How States and Societies Transform and Constitute One Another.* Cambridge: Cambridge UP, 2001.

———. *Strong Societies and Weak States: State-Society Relations and State Capabilities in the Third World.* Princeton: Princeton UP, 1988.

Muller, Edward, and Mitchell Seligson. "Civic Culture and Democracy: The Question of Causal Relationships." *American Political Science Review* 88 (1994).

Muslih, Muhammed. *Origins of Palestinian Nationalism.* New York: Columbia UP, 1988.

Najem, Tom Pierre. "State Power and Democratization in North Africa: Developments in Morocco, Algeria, Tunisia and Libya." In *Democratization in the Middle East: Experiences Struggles Challenges.* Ed. Amin Saikal and Abrecht Schnabel. New York: United Nations University, 2003.

Newton, Kenneth. "Trust, Social Capital, Civil Society, and Democracy." *International Political Science Review* (2001).

Newton, Kenneth, and Pippa Norris. "Confidence in Public Institutions: Faith, Culture, or Performance?" In *Disaffected Democracies: What's Troubling the Trilateral Countries?* Ed. Susan Pharr and Robert Putnam. Princeton: Princeton UP, 2000.

Nimer, Ahmad. *Green Left Weekly* 25 (Mar. 1988).

Norris, Pippa, ed. *Critical Citizens: Global Support for Democratic Governance.* Oxford: Oxford UP, 1999.

Norton, Augustus Richard, ed. *Civil Society in the Middle East.* New York: E. J. Brill, 1996.

———. "The Future of Civil Society in the Middle East." In *Toward Civil Society in the Middle East? A Primer.* Ed. Jillian Schwedler. Boulder: Lynne Rienner, 1995.

Nye, Joseph, Philip Zelikow, and David King. *Why People Don't Trust Government.* Cambridge: Harvard UP, 1997.

O'Connell, Brian. *Civil Society: Historical and Contemporary Perspectives.* New England: Tufts UP, 1999.

O'Donnell, Guillermo. "On the State, Democratization and Some Conceptual Problems: A Latin American View with Glances at Some Post Communist Countries." *World Development* 21.8 (1993).

Offe, Claus. "How Can We Trust Our Fellow Citizens?" In *Democracy and Trust.* Ed. Mark Warren. Cambridge: Cambridge UP, 1999.

Olsen, Mancur. *The Logic of Collective Action: Public Goods and the Theory of Groups.* Cambridge: Harvard UP, 1965.

Ottaway, Marina. "Democratization in Collapsed States." In *Collapsed States: The Integration and Restoration of Legitimate Authority.* Ed. William Zartman. Colorado: Lynne Reiner, 1995.

Ottaway, Marina, and Thomas Carothers, eds. *Funding Virtue: Civil Society Aid and Democracy Promotion.* Washington, DC: Carnegie Endowment for International Peace, 2000.

Palestinian Ministry of Higher Education. "Facts and Figures." n.d. Retrieved 11 Aug. 2002. http://www.mohe.gov.ps/ main/Factsfgrs.htm.

Palestine Monitor. http://www.palestinemonitor.org/factsheet/settlement.html.

"Petition-20." Nov. 1999. Statement issued by twenty well-known Palestinian personalities, nine of whom were Palestinian Legislative Council (PLC) members.

Pharr, Susan. "Officials Misconduct and Public Distrust: Japan and the Trilateral Democracies." In *Disaffected Democracies.* Ed. Susan Pharr and Robert Putnam. Princeton: Princeton UP, 2000.

Pharr, Susan, and Robert Putnam, eds. *Disaffected Democracies: What's Troubling the Trilateral Countries?* Princeton: Princeton UP, 2000.

Piatonni, Simona. *Clientelism, Interests, and Democratic Representation.* Cambridge: Cambridge UP, 2001.

Pitner, Julia. "NGOs Dilemmas." *Middle East Report* (2000).

"Political Rights and Censorship in Jordan: 'A Policeman on My Chest, a Scissor in My Brain.'" *MERIP Middle East Report* 0.149 (1987).

Powell, John Duncan. "Peasant Society and Clientelistic Politics." *American Political Science Review* (June 1970).

Pripstein, Marsha. "Globalization and Labor Protection in Oil Poor Countries." *Global Social Policy* 3.3 (2003).

Przeworski, Adam. *Democracy and the Market: Political and Economic Reforms in Eastern Europe and Latin America.* Cambridge: Cambridge UP, 1991.

Putnam, Robert. *Bowling Alone: The Collapse and Revival of American Community.* New York: Simon and Schuster, 2000.

———. *The Comparative Study of Political Elites.* Upper Saddle River: Prentice-Hall, 1976.

———. *Making Democracy Work.* Princeton: Princeton UP, 1993.

Qamhawi, Labib Al. "Muwaqaat wa-al-Tahadiyat fi Wajh Masirat al-Mujtama' al-Madani wa-Malamih wa Tuwajuhat Awlawiyya Liltaghyi" (The Future of The Civil Life in the Palestinian Self-Ruled Territories). In *Mustaqbal al-haya al-Madani fi manatiq ālHukm al-zati al-Filastiniyya.* Ed. Khalil Darwish. Amman: Middle East Studies Centre, 1998.

Rahman, Maha Abdel. "The Politics of 'Uncivil' Society in Egypt." *Review of African Political Economy* 91 (2002).

Riley, Dylan. "Civic Association and Authoritarian Regimes in Interwar Europe: Italy and Spain in Comparative Perspective. *American Sociological Review* (2005).

Robinson, Glenn. *Building a Palestinian State: The Incomplete Revolution.* Bloomington: Indiana UP, 1979.

———. "The Politics of Legal Reform in Palestine." *Journal of Palestine Studies* (Autumn 1997).

———. "The Role of the Professional Middle Class in the Mobilization of Palestinian Society: The Medical and Agricultural Committees." *International Journal of Middle East Studies* 25 (1993).

Roniger, Luis, and Ayse Gunes-Ataya. *Democracy, Clientelism, and Civil Society.* Boulder: Lynne Reinner, 1994.

Rose-Ackerman, Susan. *Corruption and Government: Causes, Consequences, and Reform.* Cambridge: Cambridge UP, 1999.

Rosenblum, Nancy. *Membership and Morals: The Personal Uses of Pluralism in America.* Princeton: Princeton UP, 1998.

Rosenstone, Steven, and John Hansen. *Mobilization, Participation, and Democracy in America.* New York: Macmillan, 1993.

Roy, Sara. "Gaza: New Dynamics of Civic Disintegration." *Journal of Palestine Studies* 23.3 (Spring 1994).

———. "Palestinian Society and Economy: The Continued Denial of Possibility." *Journal of Palestine Studies* 20.4 (2001).

———. "The Transformation of Islamic NGOs in Palestine." *Middle East Report* 214 (2000).

Rubin, Barry. *The Transformation of Palestinian Politics: From Revolution to State-Building.* Cambridge: Harvard UP, 1999.

Ryan, Curtis, and Jillian Schwedler. "The Return to Elections or New Hybrid Regime? The 2003 Elections in Jordan." *Middle East Policy* (Summer 2004).

Sahliyeh, Emile. *In Search of Leadership: West Bank Politics since 1967.* Washington, DC: Brookings Institute, 1998.

Salame, Ghassan, ed. *Democracy without Democrats? The Renewal of Politics in the Muslim World.* New York: I. B. Tauris, 1994.

Salim, Walid. *al-Munazamat al-Mujtama' al-Ta'wwanivya wa-al-Sultah al-Wataniyya al-Filistiniyya (Civic and Voluntary Organizations and the Palestinian National Authority).* Ramallah: MAS, 1999.

Samara, Adel. "Globalization, the Palestinian Economy and the Society since Oslo." *Journal of Palestine Studies* 33.3, 2000.

Sater, James. "Civil Society, Political Change and the Private Sector in Morocco." *Mediterranean Politics* 7.2 (Summer 2002).

Schlumberger, Oliver. "The Arab Middle East and the Question of Democratization: Some Critical Remarks." *Democratization* 7.4 (Winter 2000).

Schwedler, Jillian, ed. *Toward Civil Society in the Middle East? A Primer.* Colorado: Lynne Rienner, 1995.

Seligson, Amber. "Civic Associations and Democratic Participation in Central America." *Comparative Political Studies* 32.3 (1999).

Shaban, Radwan. "The Harsh Reality of Closure." In *Development under Adversity: The Palestinian Economy in Transition.* Ed. Ishac Diwan and Radwan Shaban. Washington, D.C.: The World Bank, 1999.

Shain, Yossi, and Gary Sussman. "From Opposition to State-Building: Palestinian Political Society Meets Palestinian Civil Society." *Government and Opposition* 33.3 (1998).

Shils, Edward. "The Virtue of Civil Society." *Government and Opposition* 26.1 (1991).

Singerman, Diane. *Avenues of Participation: Family, Politics, and Networks in Urban Quarters of Cairo.* Princeton: Princeton UP, 1995.

———. "The Politics of Emergency Rule in Egypt." *Current History* 101 (Jan. 2002).

Sivan, Emmanuel. "Arabs and Democracy: Illusions of Change." *Journal of Democracy* 11.3 (2000).

Shikaki, Khalil. "The Future of Palestine." *Foreign Affairs* (Nov./Dec.): 2004.

Skocpol, Theda, and Morris Fiorina, eds. *Civic Engagement in American Democracy.* New York: Brookings/Russell Sage Foundation, 1999.

Slymovics, Susan. "A Truth Commission for Morocco." *Middle East Report Online* 218 (Spring 2001). http://www.merip.org/mer/mer218/218_slymovics.html.

Soltan, Karol Edward. "Introduction: Citizen Competence, Democracy, and the Good Society." In *Citizen Competence and Democratic Institutions.* Ed. Stephen Elkin and Karol Edward Soltan. University Park: Pennsylvania State UP, 1999.

Sontag, Deborah. "Panel Criticizes Extent to Arafat's Power." *New York Times,* June 29, 1999.

Sourani, Raji. "Human Rights Work since Oslo: A Two Dimensional Approach." Palestine Center Briefing, Palestine Center, Washington, DC, 2000.

Stacher, Joshua. "A Democracy with Fangs and Claws and Its Effect on Egyptian Political Culture." *Arab Studies Quarterly* 23.3 (Summer 2001).

Stetter, Stephan. "Democratization without Democracy? The Assistance of European Union for Democratization Processes in Palestine." *Mediterranean Politics* 8.2–3 (2003).

Sullivan, Dennis. "NGOs in Palestine: Agents of Development and Foundation of Civil Society." *Journal of Palestine Studies* 25.3 (1996).

Tamari, Salim. "Palestinian Social Transformation: The Emergence of Civil Society." *Civil Society* 8.86 (1999). Khaldun Research Essay (23 Mar. 2000).

Taraki, Liza. "Mass Organizations in the West Bank." In *Occupation: Israel over Palestine.* Ed. Nasir Aruri. Belmont: Association of Arab-American University Graduates, 1983.

Tilly, Charles. *From Mobilization to Revolution.* New York: McGraw-Hill, 1978.

Tocqueville, Alexis de. *Democracy in America.* Ed. Richard D. Heffner. New York: New American Library, 1956.

Tvedt, Terje. *Angels of Mercy or Development Diplomats? NGOs and Foreign Aid.* Trenton: Africa World Press, 1998.

Ulsaner, Eric. "Democracy and Social Capital." In *Democracy and Trust.* Ed. Mark Warren. Cambridge: Cambridge UP, 1999.

———. *Social Capital and Participation in Everyday Life.* New York: Routledge, 2001.

United Nations Development Program (UNDP). http://www.pogar.org/countries/finances.asp?cid=12.

USAID report. http://www.abtassoc.com/reports/2002601089183_30950.pdf.

Usher, Graham. *Palestine in Crisis: The Struggle for Peace and Political Independence after Oslo.* London: Pluto Press, 1995.

*US News and World Report,* 26 Apr. 1993.

Verba, Sydney. *Elites and the Idea of Equality: A Comparison of Japan, Sweden and the United States.* Cambridge: Harvard UP, 1987.

Verba, Sydney, Norman H. Nie, and Jae-On Kim. *Participation and Political Equality: A Seven-Nation Comparison.* Chicago: The U of Chicago Press, 1978.

Verba, Sydney, Kay Lehman Schlozman, and Henry Brady. *Voice and Equality.* Cambridge: Harvard UP, 1995.

Waltzer, Michael. "The Civil Society Argument." In *Dimensions of Radical Democracy: Pluralism, Citizenship, Community.* Ed. Chantel Mouffe. New York: Verso, 1992.

Warren, Mark. *Democracy and Association.* Princeton: Princeton UP, 2001.

———. ed. *Democracy and Trust.* Cambridge: Cambridge UP, 1999.

Watanuki, Joji. *Politics in Postwar Japanese Society.* Tokyo: U of Tokyo Press, 1977.

Waterbury, John. "Endemic and Planned Corruption in a Monarchical Regime." *World Politics* 25.4 (1973).

Weber, Max. *Economy and Society: An Outline of Interpretive Sociology.* Ed. Guenther Roth and Claus Wittich. Berkeley: U of California Press, 1968.

White, Gregory. "The Advent of Electoral Democracy in Morocco? The Referendum of 1996." *Middle East Journal* 51.3 (1997).

Wiktorowicz, Quintan. "State Power and the Regulation of Islam in Jordan." *Journal of Church and State.* 41.4 (1999).

World Bank. "New Paths to Social Development: Community and Global Networks in Action." Working Paper 22339, 31 May 2000. Retrieved 8 Aug. 2002. http://www-wds.worldbank.org/servlet/WDS_IBank_Servlet?pcont=details&eid=000094946_01061904015428.

———. *West Bank and Gaza: Country Brief.* Washington, DC: World Bank, Aug. 2000.

Wuthnow, Robert. "The Role of Trust in Civic Renewal." In *Civil Society, Democracy, and Civic Renewal.* Ed. Robert Fullinwider. New York: Rowman and Littlefield, 1999.

Zartman, William, ed. *Collapsed States: The Disintegration and Restoration of Legitimate Authority.* Boulder: Lynne Rienner, 1995.

———. ed. *Elites in the Modern Middle East.* New York: Praeger, 1980.

Zubaida, Sami. "Islam in Contemporary Egypt: Civil Society vs. the State." *American Political Science Review* 95.1 (Mar. 2001).

# Index

Abd al-Shaf'i Ghassan al-Khatib, Haydar, 39
Abdullah II bin al-Hussein (king of Jordan), 117
Abu Meiden, Freih, 68
Abu Saeda, Hafez, 125
Abu Ziyadah, 40
accountability: in Arab states, 16–17; in authoritarian contexts, 16–17, 26; civic organizations and state, 5; in democracies, 2, 17, 25–26; Israel as legitimized by demands for PNA, 72; of PNA, 44, 67, 72, 77; trust and, 77, 127; in West Bank, 24
Administrative Autonomy, 32–33, 34
anti-PNA associations: corruption rather than ideology reason for opposition to PNA, 57, 59–60, 90–91, 136; democratic orientation of, 59–60, 71n52, 88–89, 92, 131–32, 134; donor aid and, 67, 69–74, 73–74; engagement levels and, 50, 90–92, 131–32; excluded from clientelistic networks, 50–51, 57–58, 81, 90; Fatah and, 58; funding of, 66, 67, 69–70; horizontal organizational structure of, 81, 88, 131–32; Islamist associations as, 90; licensing requirement and, 68; membership in, 19, 93; national identity and, 132; Oslo Accords opposed by, 61–62, 67; as pragmatic and locally focused, 74; programs linked to political agenda of, 49; reforms as objective of, 91–92, 132, 136; resource limitations of, 66, 136–37; self-selection and membership in, 93; socialization and learning within, 132; trust and, 80, 90–92, 131–32, 134
Aqsa Intifada (2000-2004), 10, 46
Arab Executive Committee, 30
Arab states: accountability in, 16–17; authoritarian orientation in, 26; democracy in, 12–13; Palestinian-Israeli negotiations as low priority for, 48; state-centralized clientelism in, 14–16, 19. *See also specific nations*
Arafat, Yasir: Area A as controlled by, 28; authoritarian governing style of, 11–12,

23–24, 37, 39–44, 46, 49; Basic Law rejected by, 43, 45; clientelism and patronage used by, 11–12, 37, 39, 54, 55–56, 58; consolidation of political power by, 23–24, 42–43, 47, 69; death of, 22; democratic reforms resisted by, 43–44, 46, 60–61, 67; Fatah and, 39, 46, 58; Gulf War support of Hussein by, 61–62; Hamas as political threat to, 69; High State Security Court created by, 45–46; leftist organizations and opposition to policies of, 36–37; limitations of power of, 23; loyalty to leadership of, 60, 66; media controlled by, 25n7, 44; Oslo Accords and leadership of, 64; PLC's political authority rejected by, 43–44; as PLO leader, 28, 36–37, 43; polarization as response to leadership style of, 40–41; return of from exile, 37; supporters of, 39; U.S. opposition to, 22, 23
Areas A, B, and C, 28; map of, 29
A'shrawi, Hanan, 39, 46
associational life: bureaucracy as barrier to activism, 124; clientelism and typology of, 80; in Egypt, 118, 123–24; in Jordan, 115–17, 120–23; in Morocco, 107, 115; Oslo Accords as context for, 13; polarization of, 14, 115–17, 122–23; in post-Oslo period, 36–41; social capital and, 4, 5, 85, 129; Western democracies as context for, 3–10. *See also* West Bank civic associations
authoritarianism: accountability lacking in, 16–17, 26; Arab Middle East as inclined toward, 26; Arafat's governing style as authoritarian, 11–12, 23–24, 37, 39–44, 46, 49; civic organization as constraint on, 5; civic sphere co-opted by, 116; as context for civic associations, 13, 21, 24–25, 77; in developing world, 21; in Egypt, 117–18; employment opportunity as control mechanism in, 122; engagement and, 77, 81; external or radical threats as rationale for, 12, 47, 124; information economy